TENNIS RULES ILLUSTRATED

TENNIS RULES ILLUSTRATED

Edited by George Sullivan

Produced by Charles Fellows

CORNERSTONE LIBRARY
Published by Simon & Schuster
NEW YORK

Published by Cornerstone Library
A Simon & Schuster Division of
Gulf & Western Corporation
1230 Avenue of the Americas
New York, New York 10020

Library of Congress Cataloging in Publication Data

Sullivan, George, 1927–
Tennis rules illustrated.

1. Tennis—Rules. I. Title.
GV1001.S94 796.342' 02' 022 80-27725

ISBN 0-346-12525-1

Manufactured in the
United States of America

10 9 8 7 6 5 4 3 2 1

The Rules of Tennis are reprinted
by permission of the United States
Tennis Association.

INTRODUCTION

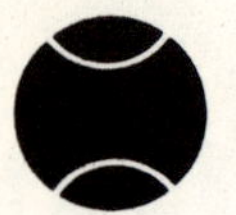

INTRODUCTION

In December 1873 at a garden party at Nantclwyd in Wales, Major Walter C. Wingfield, a British Army officer, introduced a game he called "Sphairistike or Lawn Tennis." The major intended to patent the game, and sell the rules, court diagrams, and nets, rackets, and other equipment.

But the game that Major Wingfield claimed to have invented was hardly an original item. He drew heavily upon the badminton, rackets, and the ancient game of court tennis.

The net in the major's game was almost 5 feet high (compared to the 3 foot net of modern tennis), a concept drawn from badminton. The provision for a 15-point game and the idea that only the server could score were common to rackets. The court with two sides divided by a net was derived from court tennis. A tennis historian has called the major's original rulebook a "goulash."

Within a year, the major reheated the mixture. His 1874 edition of the rules provided for serving from either side of the net. Previously, only one side had been designated as the serving side. In the original rules, the game's service courts had been—badmintonlike—at the rear of the court. For 1874, the major moved them up to the front part, near the net, and established that the server had to be at the baseline.

Even before the major had an opportunity to revise the rules, his game was on its way to international popularity. A military officer at the major's party where the pioneer game was played became so enthusiastic about it that, two weeks later when he embarked for Bermuda, he took a supply of balls and rackets with him and had a net constructed when he arrived.

The military officer had hardly finished introducing the sport to his colleagues when an American woman—Mary Ewing Outerbridge of Staten Island, New York—arrived in Bermuda on a vacation. After she watched the game being played, she felt it was one that could be enjoyed by her friends back home. When she sailed for New York in March 1874, she carried tennis equipment with her. Her brother, A. Emilius Outerbridge, got her permission to set up a net and mark out a court on the grounds of the Staten Island Cricket and Baseball Club.

Within a few years, the game was being played in New York, Boston, and Philadelphia. But there was enormous confusion over the rules. The size and weight of the balls, the height of the net, and the system of scoring were in dispute almost everywhere. Finally, on May 21, 1881, the Eastern clubs where tennis was played sent representatives to a meeting in New York City to standardize the rules.

In the meantime, tennis had become popular in England as a club game and at private estates. Wingfield's rules were constantly being tinkered with. The hourglass shape for the court, which Wingfield had specified, was changed to a rectangle. The net was made lower. The court-tennis system of games and sets was introduced.

In 1877, when the All-England Croquet and Tennis Club held the first All-England Tournament at Wimbledon, where the club was located, it was these rules that governed play. And four years later, when American club representatives met in New York to standardize play, they agreed to adopt the All-England rules. They served as the basis of the modern rules of tennis, set down on the pages that follow.

Major Walter Clopton Wingfield, M.V.O.

OFFICIAL RULES OF TENNIS

THE SINGLES GAME

RULE 1

Dimensions and Equipment

The court shall be a rectangle 78 feet (23.77 meters) long and 27 feet (8.23 meters) wide. It shall be divided across the middle by a net suspended from a cord or metal cable of a maximum diameter of one-third of an inch (0.8 centimeters), the ends of which shall be attached to, or pass over, the tops of two posts, 3 feet 6 inches (1.07 meters) high, and not more than 6 inches (15 centimeters) in diameter, the centers of which shall be 3 feet (0.91 meters) outside the court on each side.

The net shall be extended fully so that it fills completely the space between the two posts and shall be of sufficiently small mesh to prevent the ball's passing through. The height of the net shall be 3 feet (0.914 meters) at the center where it shall be held down taut by a strap not more than 2 inches (5 centimeters) wide and white in color.

There shall be band covering the cord or metal cable and the top of the net for not less than 2 inches (5 centimeters) nor more than 2 1/2 inches (6.3 centimeters) in depth on each side and white in color. There shall be no advertisement on the net, strap, band or singles sticks.

The lines bounding the ends and sides of the Court shall respectively be called the Baselines and the Sidelines. On each side of the net, at a distance of 21 feet (6.40 meters) from it and parallel with it, shall be drawn the service lines. The space on each side of the net between the service line and the sidelines shall be divided into two equal parts, called the service courts, by the center service line, which must be 2 inches (5 centimeters) in width, drawn half-way between, and parallel with, the sidelines.

Each baseline shall be bisected by an imaginary continuation of the center service line to a line 4 inches (10 centimeters) in length and 2 inches (5 centimeters) in width called the center mark, drawn inside the Court at right angles to and in contact with such baselines.

All other lines shall be not less than 1 inch (2.5 centimeters) nor more than 2 inches (5 centimeters) in width, except the baseline, which may be 4 inches (10 centimeters) in width, and all measurements shall be made to the outside of the lines.

RULE 2

Permanent Fixtures

The permanent fixtures of the Court shall include not only the net posts, cord or metal cable, strap and band, but also, where there are any such, the back and side stops, the stands, fixed or movable seats and chairs around the Court, and their occupants, all other fixtures around and above the Court, and the Chair Umpire, Net Umpire, Line Umpires and Ball Boys when in their respective places.

RULE 3

Ball—Size, Weight and Bound

The ball shall have a uniform outer surface and shall be white or yellow in color. If there are any seams they shall be stitchless.

The ball shall be more than two and a half inches (6.35 centimeters) and less than two and five-eighths inches (6.67 centimeters) in diameter, and more than two ounces (56.7 grams) and less than two and one-sixteenth ounces (58.5 grams) in weight.

The ball shall have a bound of more than 53 inches (135 centimeters) and less than 58 inches (147 centimeters) when dropped 100 inches (254 centimeters) upon a concrete base.

The ball shall have a forward deformation of more than .220 of an inch (.56 centimeters) and less than .290 of an inch (.74 centimeters) and a return deformation of more than .350 of an inch (.89 centimeters) and less than .425 of an inch (1.08 centimeters) at 18 lbs. (8.165 kilograms) load. The two deformation figures shall be the averages of three individual readings along three axes of the ball and no two individual readings shall differ by more than .030 of an inch (.08 centimeters) in each case.

Regulations for conducting tests for bound, size and deformation of balls may be found on page 515 of the 1979 USTA Yearbook or obtained from USTA in New York.

RULE 4

The Racket

The racket shall consist of a frame and a stringing. The frame may be of any material, weight, size or shape.

The strings must be alternately interlaced or bonded where they cross, and each string must be connected to the frame. If there

SINGLES COURT

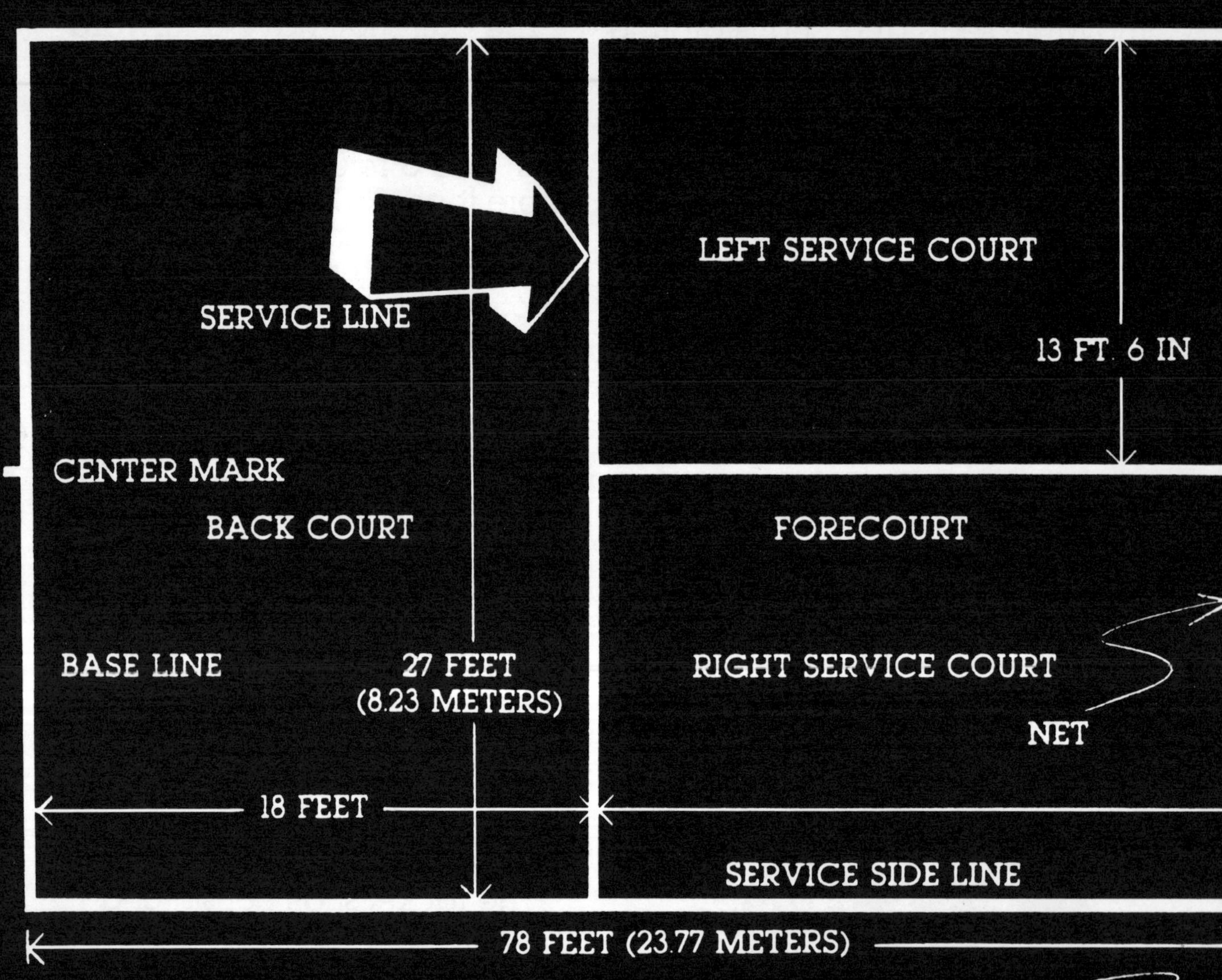

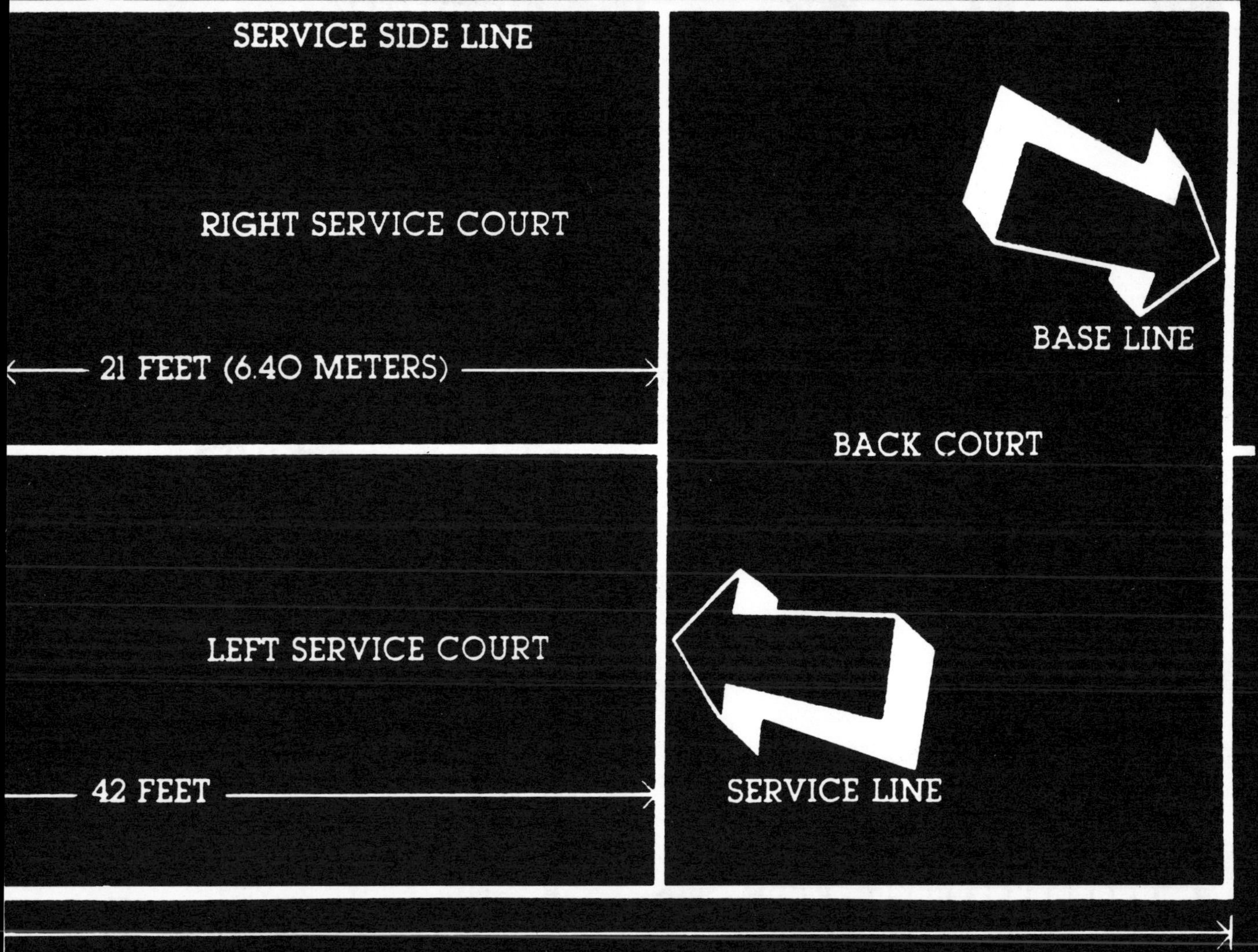

SERVICE SIDE LINE

RIGHT SERVICE COURT

BASE LINE

← 21 FEET (6.40 METERS) →

BACK COURT

LEFT SERVICE COURT

— 42 FEET →

SERVICE LINE

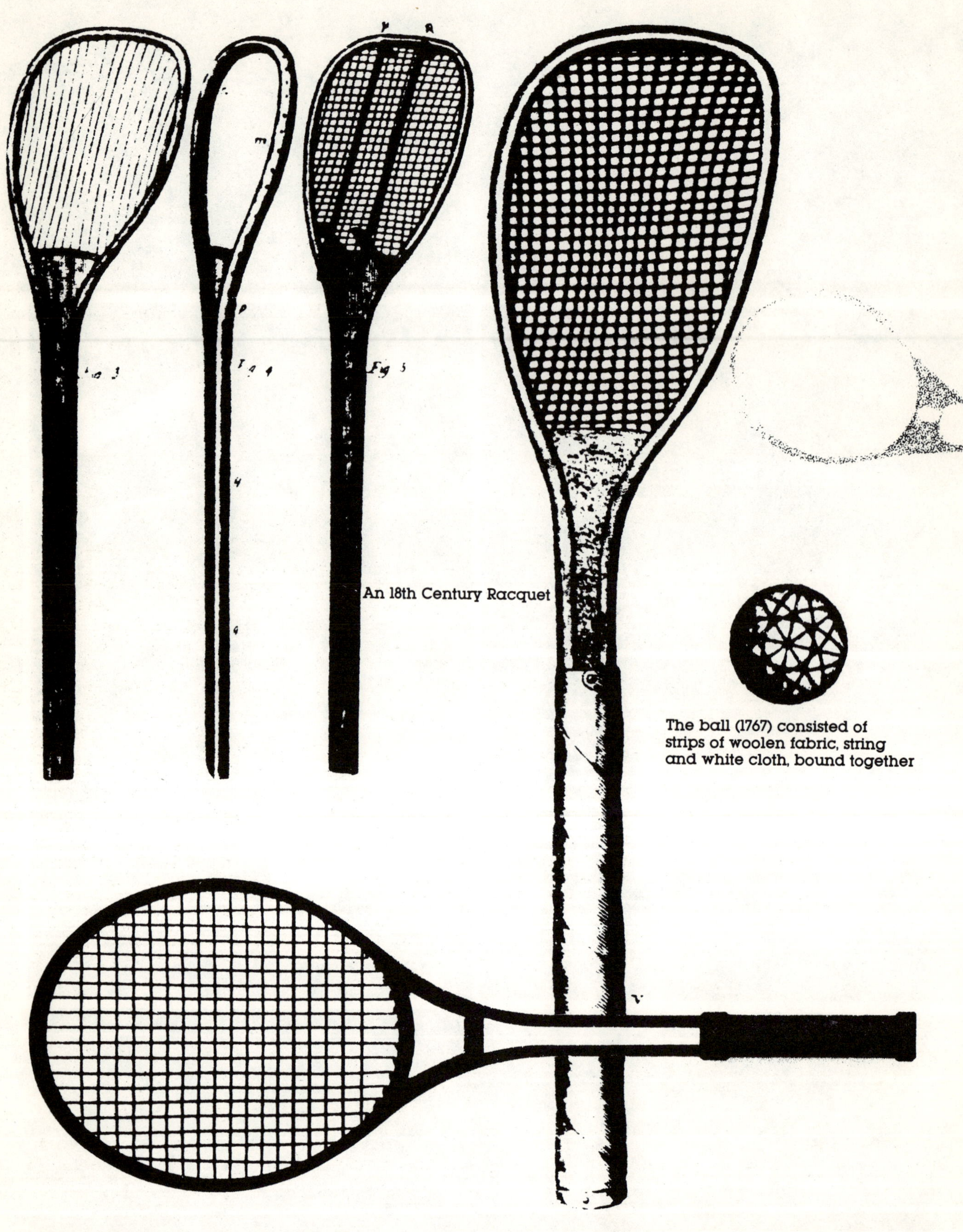

An 18th Century Racquet

The ball (1767) consisted of strips of woolen fabric, string and white cloth, bound together

are attachments, they must be used only to prevent wear and tear and must not alter the flight of the ball. The density in the center must be at least equal to the average density of the stringing. The stringing must be made so that the moves between the strings will not exceed that which is possible, for instance, with 18 mains and 18 crosses uniformly spaced and interlaced in a stringing area of 75 square inches.

RULE 5

Server and Receiver

The players shall stand on opposite sides of the net; the player who first delivers the ball shall be called the Server, and the other the Receiver.

RULE 6

Choice of Ends and Service

The choice of ends and the right to be a Server or Receiver in the first game shall be decided by toss. The player winning the toss may choose, or require his opponent to choose.

(a) The right to be Server or Receiver, in which case the other player shall choose the end, or

(b) The end, in which case the other player shall choose the right to be Server or Receiver.

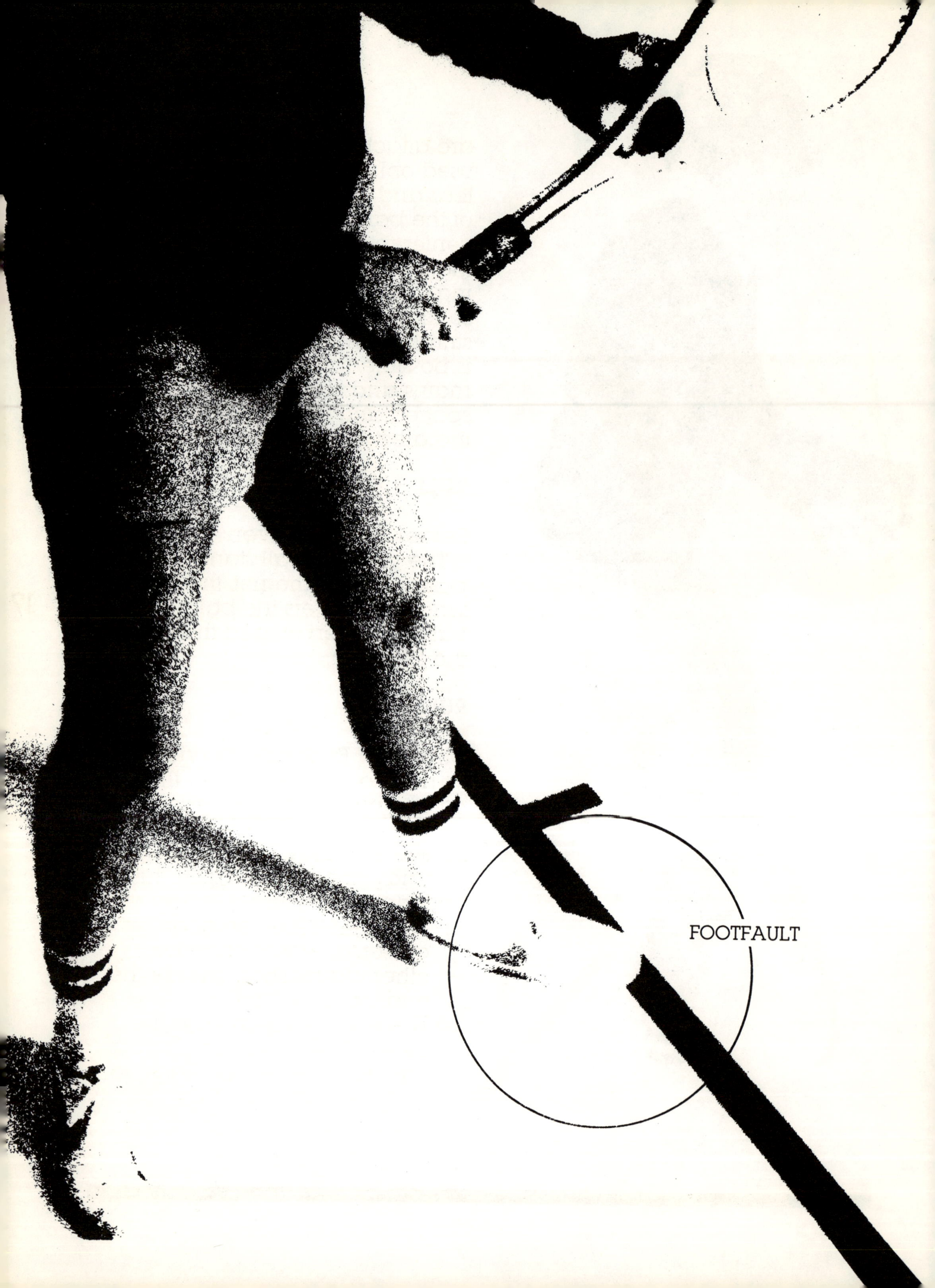
FOOTFAULT

RULE 7

Delivery of Service

The service shall be delivered in the following manner. Immediately before commencing to serve, the Server shall stand with both feet at rest behind (i.e. farther from the net than) the base-line, and within the imaginary continuations of the center-mark and side-line. The Server shall then project the ball by hand into the air in any direction and before it hits the ground strike it with his racket. The delivery shall be deemed to have been completed at the moment of the impact of the racket and the ball. A player with the use of only one arm may utilize his racket for the projection.

RULE 8

Foot Fault

The Server shall throughout the delivery of the service:

(a) Not change his position by walking or running.

(b) Not touch, with either foot, any area other than that behind the baseline within the imaginary extension of the center-mark and sideline.

RULE 9

From Alternate Courts

(a) In delivering the service, the Server shall stand alternately behind the right and left Courts, beginning from the right in every game. If service from a wrong half of the Court occurs and is undetected, all play resulting from such wrong service or services shall stand, but the inaccuracy of the station shall be corrected immediately when it is discovered.

(b) The ball served shall pass over the net and hit the ground within the Service Court which is diagonally opposite, or upon any line bounding such Court, before the Receiver returns it.

RULE 10

Faults

The Service is a fault:

(a) If the Server commits any breach of Rules 7, 8 or 9;

(b) If he misses the ball in attempting to strike it;

(c) If the ball served touches a permanent fixture (other than the net, strap or band) before it hits the ground.

CENTER MARK

If a player when serving throws up two or more balls instead of one, a let should be called. But if the umpire regards the action as deliberate he may take action under Rule 21.

RULE 11

Service After a Fault

After a fault (if it be the first fault) the Server shall serve again from behind the same half of the Court from which he served that fault, unless the service was from the wrong half, when, in accordance with Rule 9, the Server shall be entitled to one Service only from behind the other half. A fault may be claimed after the next service has been delivered.

RULE 12

Receiver Must Be Ready

The Server shall not serve until the Receiver is ready. If the latter attempts to return the service, he shall be deemed ready. If, however, the Receiver signifies that he is not ready, he may not claim a fault because the ball does not hit the ground within the limits for the service.

RULE 13

A Let

In all cases where a let has to be called under the rules, or to provide for an interruption to play, it shall have the following interpretations:

(a) When called solely in respect of a service, that one service only shall be replayed.

(b) When called under any circumstance, the point shall be replayed.

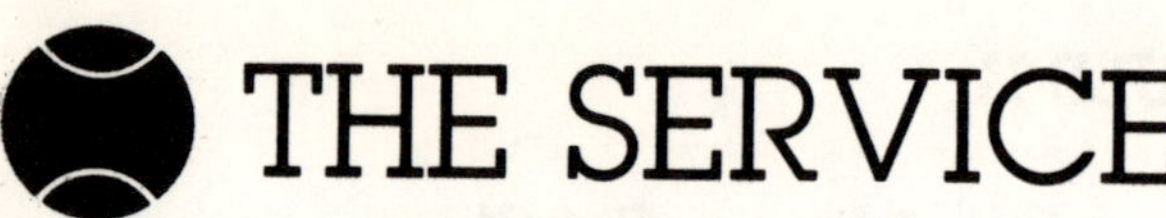

THE SERVICE

1 Assume the Proper Stance

2 Don't Rush the Toss

UNWRITTEN RULES

3 Racquet Back

4 Hit the Ball at the Highest Possible Point

5 **Follow Through on the Opposite Side of the Body**

RULE 14

The Service Is A Let

The service is a let:

(a) If the ball served touches the net, strap or band, and is otherwise good, or, after touching the net, strap or band, touches the Receiver or anything which he wears or carries before hitting the ground.

(b) If a service or a fault is delivered when the Receiver is not ready (see Rule 12).

In case of a let, that particular service shall not count, and the Server shall serve again, but a service does not annul a previous fault.

RULE 15

When Receiver Becomes Server

At the end of the first game the Receiver shall become the Server, and the Server, Receiver; and so on alternately in all the subsequent games of a match. If a player serves out of turn, the player who ought to have served shall serve as soon as the mistake is discovered, but all points scored before such discovery shall be reckoned. If a game shall have been completed before such discovery, the order of service remains as altered. A fault served before such discovery shall not be reckoned.

RULE 16

When Players Change Ends

The players shall change ends at the end of the first, third and every subsequent alternate game of each set, and at the end of each set unless the total number of games in such set be even, in which case the change is not made until the end of the first game of the next set.

If a mistake is made and the correct sequence is not followed the players must take up their correct station as soon as the discovery is made and follow their original sequence.

RULE 17

Ball In Play Till Point Decided

A ball is in play from the moment at which it is delivered in service. Unless a fault or let be called, it remains in play until the point is decided.

RULE 18

Server Wins Point

The Server wins the Point:

(a) If the ball served, not being a let under Rule 14, touches the Receiver or anything which he wears or carries, before it hits the ground.

(b) If the Receiver otherwise loses the point as provided by Rule 20.

RULE 19

Receiver Wins Point

The Receiver wins the point:

(a) If the Server serves two consecutive faults;

(b) If the Server otherwise loses the point as provided by Rule 20.

RULE 20

Player Loses Point

A player loses the point if:

(a) He fails, before the ball in play has hit the ground twice consecutively, to return it directly over the net, except as provided in Rule 24 (a) or (c); or

(b) He returns the ball in play so well it hits the ground, a permanent fixture, or other object, outside any of the lines which bound his opponent's Court, except as provided in Rule 24 (a) or (c); or

(c) He volleys the ball and fails to make a good return even when standing outside the Court; or

(d) In playing the ball he deliberately carries it or catches it on his racket or deliberately touches it with his racket more than once; or

(e) He or his racket (in his hand or otherwise) or anything which he wears or carries touch the net, post (single stick, if they are in use), cord or metal cable, strap or band, or the ground within his opponent's

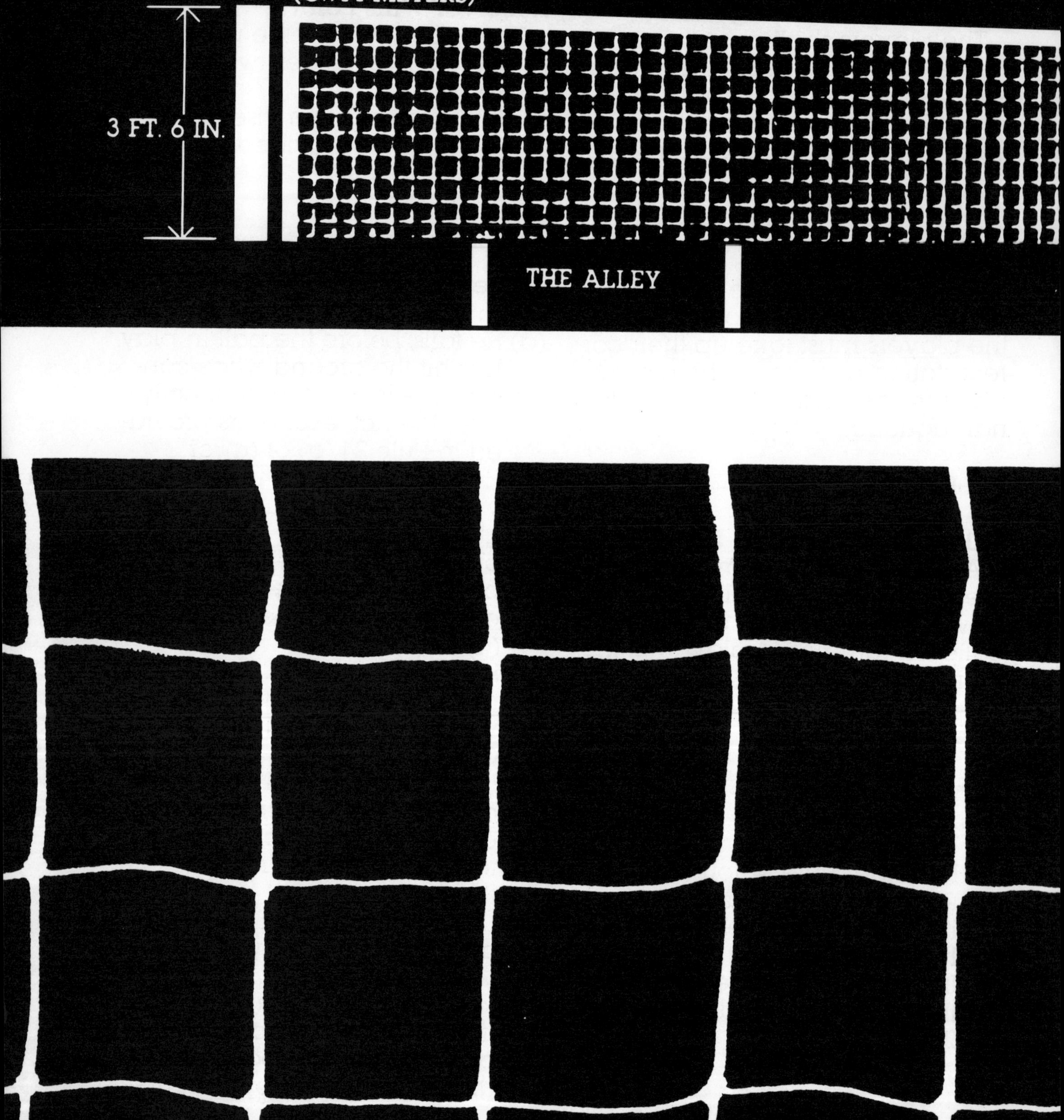
(0.91 METERS)
3 FT. 6 IN.
THE ALLEY

NET

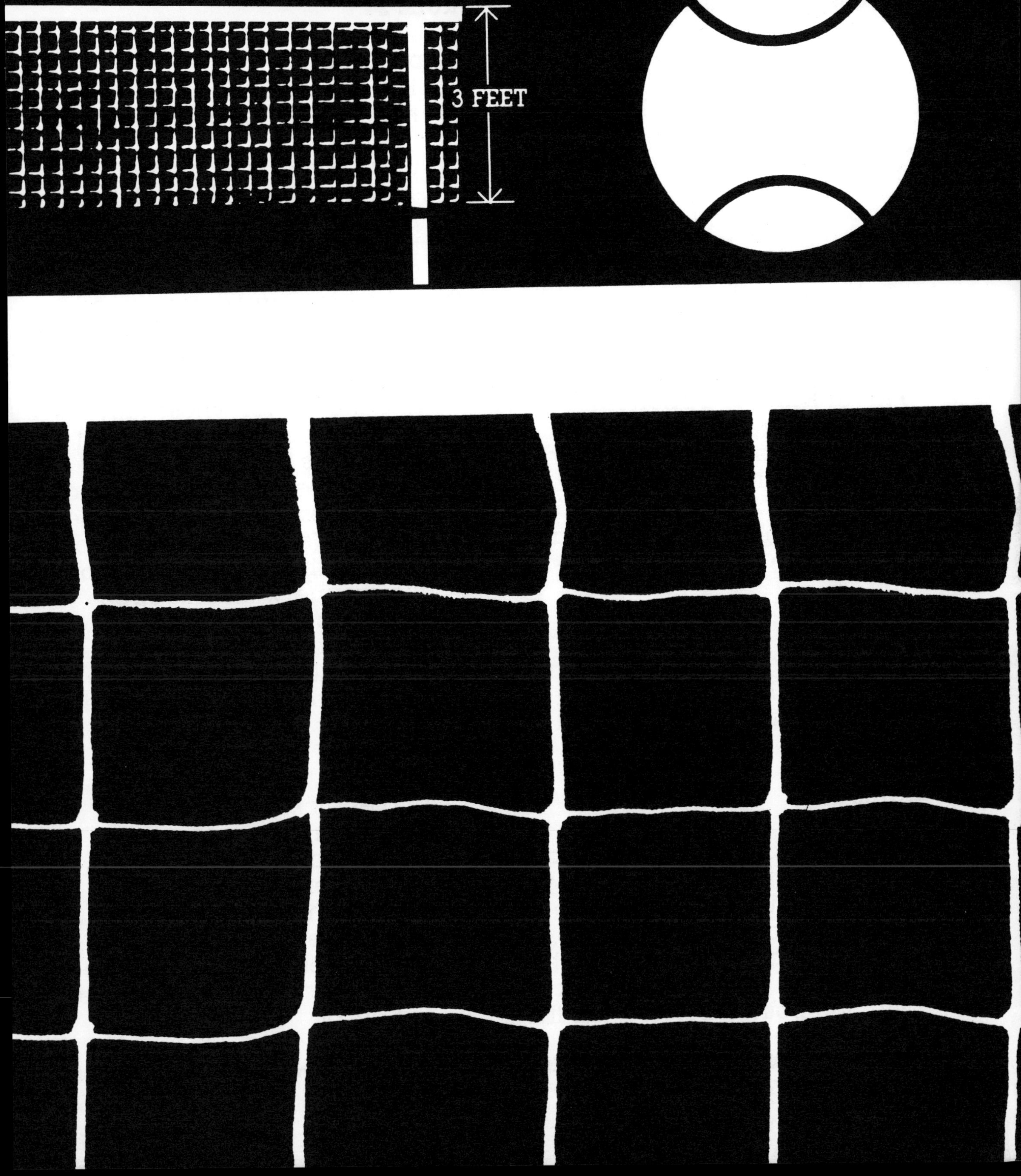

3 FEET

Court at any time while the ball is in play (touching a pipe support running across the court at the bottom of the net is interpreted as touching the net); (See Note at Rule 23); or

(f) He volleys the ball before it has passed the net; or

(g) The ball in play touches him or anything that he wears or carries, except his racket in his hand or hands; or

(h) He throws his racket at and hits the ball.

RULE 21

Player Hinders Opponent

If a player commits any act which hinders his opponent in making a stroke, then, if this is deliberate, he shall lose the point or if involuntary, the point shall be replayed.

RULE 22

Ball Falling on Line—Good

A ball falling on a line is regarded as falling in the Court bounded by that line.

RULE 23

Ball Touching Permanent Fixture

If the ball in play touches a permanent fixture (other than the net, posts, cord or metal cable, strap or band) after it has hit the ground, the player who struck it wins the point; if before it hits the ground, his opponent wins the point.

RULE 24

Good Return

It is a good return:

(a) If the ball touches the net, post (singles stick, if they are in use), cord or metal cable, strap or band, provided that it passes over any of them and hits the ground within the Court; or

(b) If the ball, served or returned, hits the ground within the proper Court and rebounds or is blown back over the net, and the player whose turn it is to strike reaches over the net and plays the ball, provided that neither he nor any part of his clothes or racket touch the net, post (singles stick), cord or metal cable, strap or band or the ground within his opponent's Court, and that the stroke is otherwise good; or

(c) If the ball is returned outside the post or singles stick, either above or below the level of the top of the net, even though it touches the post or singles stick, provided that it hits the ground within the proper Court; or

(d) If a player's racket passes over the net after he has returned the ball, provided the ball passes the net before being played and is properly returned; or

(e) If a player succeeds in returning the ball, served or in play, which strikes a ball lying in the Court (i.e. on his court when the point started).

RULE 25

Interference

In case a player is hindered in making a stroke by anything not within his control except a permanent fixture of the Court, or except as provided for in Rule 21, the point shall be replayed.

RULE 26

The Game

If a player wins his first point, the score is called 15 for that player; on winning his second point, the score is called 30 for that player; on winning his third point, the score is called 40 for that player, and the fourth point won by a player is scored game for that player except as below:

If both players have won three points, the score is called deuce; and the next point won by a player is called advantage for that player. If the same player wins the next point, he wins the game; if the other player wins the next point the score is again called deuce; and so on until a player wins the two points immediately following the score at deuce, when the game is scored for that player.

RULE 27

The Set

A player (or players) who first wins six games wins a set; except that he must win by a margin of two games over his opponent and where necessary a set shall be extended until this margin be achieved.

RULE 28

Maximum Number of Sets

The maximum number of sets in a match shall be 5, or, where women take part, 3.

RULE 29

Rules Apply to Both Sexes

Except where otherwise stated, every reference in these Rules to the masculine includes the feminine gender.

RULE 30

Decisions of Umpire and Referee

In matches where a Chair Umpire is appointed, his decision shall be final; but where a Referee is appointed an appeal shall lie to him from the decision of a Chair Umpire on a question of law, and in all such cases the decision of the Referee shall be final.

In matches where assistants to the Chair Umpire are appointed (Line Umpires, Net Umpire, Footfault Judge) their decisions shall be final on questions of fact, except that if, in the opinion of the Chair Umpire, a clear mistake has been made, he shall have the right to change the decision of an assistant or order a let to be played.

When such an assistant is unable to give a decision he shall indicate this immediately to the Chair Umpire who shall give a decision. When the Chair is unable to give a decision on a question of fact he shall order a let to be played.

In Davis Cup or other team matches where a Referee is on court, any decision can be changed by the Referee, who may also instruct the Chair Umpire to order a let to be played.

The Referee, in his discretion, may at any time postpone a match on account of darkness or the condition of the ground or the weather. In any case of postponement the previous score and previous occupancy of courts shall hold good, unless the Referee and the players unanimously agree otherwise.

RULE 31

Play shall be continuous from the first service till the match is concluded:

(a) Notwithstanding the above, after the third set (or when women take part the second set) either player is entitled to a rest, which shall not exceed 10 minutes, or, in countries situated between Latitude 15 degrees north and Latitude 15 degrees south, 45 minutes, and furthermore when necessitated by circumstances not within the control of the players the Chair Umpire may suspend play for such a period as he may consider necessary.

If play is suspended and not resumed until a later day, the rest may be taken only after the third set (or when women take part the second set) of play on such later day, completion of an unfinished set being counted as one set.

If play is suspended and not resumed until 10 minutes have elapsed in the same day, the rest may be taken only after three consecutive sets have been played without interruption (or when women take part two sets), completion of an unfinished set being counted as one set.

Any nation is at liberty to modify this provision or omit it from its regulations governing tournaments, matches or competitions held in its own country, other than the International Tennis Championships (Davis Cup and Federation Cup).

(b) Play shall never be suspended, delayed or interfered with for the purpose of enabling a player to recover his strength or his breath.

(c) A maximum of 30 seconds shall elapse from the end of one point to the time the ball is served for the next point, except that when changing ends a maximum of one minute 30 seconds shall elapse from the last point of one game to the time when the ball is served for the first point of the next game.

These provisions shall be strictly construed. The Chair Umpire shall be the sole judge of any suspension, delay or interference and after giving due warning he may disqualify the offender.

RULE 32

Coaching

During a match a player may not receive any coaching or advice, except that when a player changes ends he may receive instruction from a Captain who is sitting on the Court in a team competition.

RULE 33

Ball Change Error

In cases where balls are changed after an agreed number of games, if the balls are not changed in the correct sequence the mistake shall be corrected when the player, or pair in the case of doubles, who should have served with the new balls is next due to serve.

RULE 34

The above Rules shall apply to the Doubles Game except as below.

THE DOUBLES GAME

RULE 35

Dimensions of Court

For the Doubles Game the Court shall be 36 feet (10.97 meters) in width, i.e. 4 1/2 feet (1.37 meters) wider on each side than the Court for the Singles Game, and those portions of the singles sidelines which lie between the two service lines shall be called the service sidelines. In other respects the Court shall be similar to that described in Rule 1, but the portions of the singles sidelines between the baseline and the service line on each side of the net may be omitted if desired.

RULE 36

Order of Service

The order of serving shall be decided at the beginning of each set as follows:

The pair who have to serve in the first game of each set shall

DOUBLES COURT

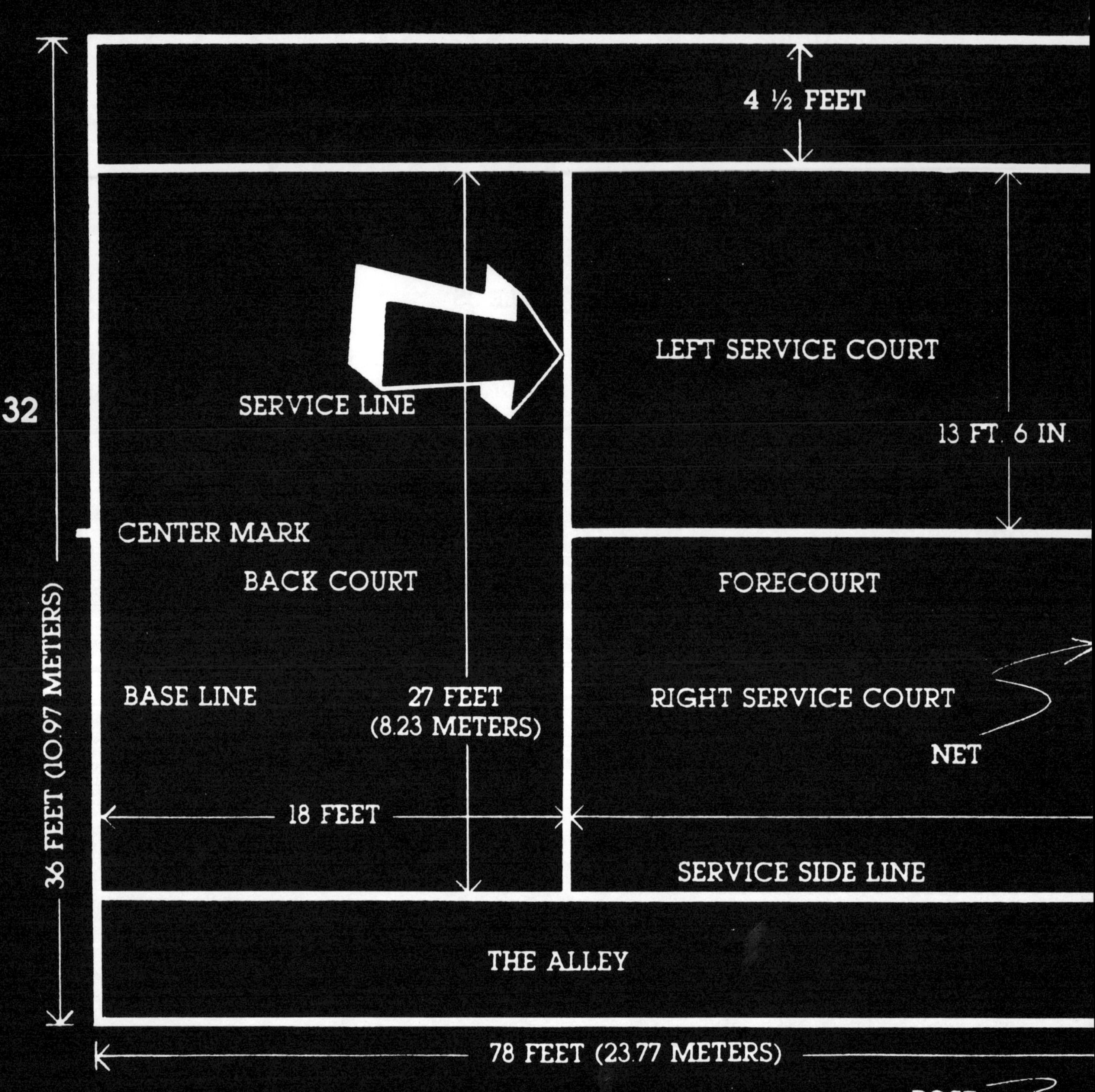

32

THE ALLEY

SERVICE SIDE LINE

RIGHT SERVICE COURT

BASE LINE

21 FEET (6.40 METERS)

BACK COURT

LEFT SERVICE COURT

SERVICE LINE

42 FEET

decide which partner shall do so and the opposing pair shall decide similarly for the second game. The partner of the player who served in the first game shall serve in the third; the partner of the player who served in the second game shall serve in the fourth, and so on in the same order in all subsequent games of a set.

RULE 37

Order of Receiving

The order of receiving the service shall be decided at the beginning of each set as follows:

The pair who have to receive the service in the first game shall decide which partner shall receive the first service, and that partner shall continue to receive the first service in every odd game, throughout the set. The opposing pair shall likewise decide which partner shall receive the first service in the second game and that partner shall continue to receive the first service in every even game throughout that set. Partners shall receive the service alternately throughout each game.

RULE 38

Service Out of Turn

If a partner serves out of his turn, the partner who ought to have served shall serve as soon as the mistake is discovered, but all points scored, and any faults served before such discovery shall be reckoned. If a game shall have been completed before such discovery the order of service remains as altered.

RULE 39

Error in Order of Receiving

If during a game the order of receiving the service is changed by the receivers it shall remain as altered until the end of the game in which the mistake is discovered, but the partners shall resume their original order of receiving in the next game of that set in which they are receivers of the service.

RULE 40

Ball Touching Server's Partner Is Fault

The service is a fault as provided for by Rule 10, or if the ball served touches the Server's partner or anything which he wears or carries, not being a let under Rule 14 (a), before it hits the ground, the Server wins the point.

RULE 41

Ball Struck Alternately

The ball shall be struck alternately by one or other player of the opposing pairs, and if a player touches the ball in play with his racket in contravention of this Rule, his opponents win the point.

HOW TO KEEP SCORE

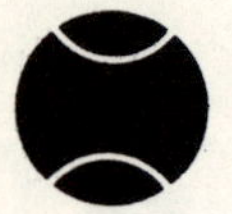

HOW TO KEEP SCORE

Billie Jean King often said that the scoring system used in tennis was a confusing one. At least for people new to the sport as spectators or for those who have never played the game, it is confusing.

To know how to keep score in tennis, you have to know the meaning of these terms: game, set, and match.

A game in tennis is scored in points. But instead of designating the points one, two, three, and so on, tennis has its own names for points

O (zero) is called love
1st point won by a player is called 15
2nd point won by a player is called 30
3rd point won by a player is called 40

The first player to win a fourth point wins the game. However, if each player wins three points (a score of 40 each), the score is termed deuce. After the score is deuce, the next point won by a player is called advantage. A player has to gain a lead of two points in order to win a game.

The first player to win six games wins a set, provided he or she is at least two games ahead of his or her opponent.

In accordance with this rule, sets sometimes used to go on and on, with neither player able to gain a two-game edge. Set scores such as 12-10 or 14-12 were sometimes recorded. Not any more. In 1970 at the U.S. Open at Forest Hills, a system of breaking ties was introduced. Later adopted by the United States Tennis Association and the International Lawn Tennis Federation, it limits all sets to a maximum of 13 games. Sometimes the tie-breaking sequence is called "sudden death."

When the set score reaches 6-all, players compete on a best-of-nine-points basis to break the tie. That is, the first player to win 5 points wins the set (by a score of 7-6).

Player A, the one who ordinarily would be going to serve the thirteenth game, serves the first two points. Player B serves the next two. They then change sides and Player A serves points 5 and 6. Player B then serves the remaining points, if necessary. The sequence ends as soon as a player wins a fifth point.

LOVE

15

30

40

GAME

USTA CHAMPIONS

USTA Men's Singles Champions

Year	Champion	Runner-up
1881	R. D. Sears	W. E. Glyn
1882	R. D. Sears	C. M. Clark
1883	R. D. Sears	J. Dwight
1884	R. D. Sears	H. A. Taylor
1885	R. D. Sears	G. M. Brinley
1886	R. D. Sears	R. L. Beeckman
1887	R. D. Sears	H. W. Slocum, Jr.
1888	H. W. Slocum, Jr.	H. A. Taylor
1889	H. W. Slocum, Jr.	Q. A. Shaw
1890	O. S. Campbell	H. W. Slocum, Jr.
1891	O. S. Campbell	C. Hobart
1892	O. S. Campbell	F. H. Hovey
1893	R. D. Wrenn	F. H. Hovey
1894	R. D. Wrenn	M. F. Goodbody
1895	F. H. Hovey	R. D. Wrenn
1896	R. D. Wrenn	F. H. Hovey
1897	R. D. Wrenn	W. V. Eaves
1898	M. D. Whitman	D. F. Davis
1899	M. D. Whitman	J. P. Paret
1900	M. D. Whitman	W. A. Larned
1901	W. A. Larned	B. C. Wright
1902	W. A. Larned	R. F. Doherty
1903	H. L. Doherty	W. A. Larned
1904	Holcombe Ward	W. J. Clothier
1905	B. C. Wright	Holcombe Ward
1906	W. J. Clothier	B. C. Wright
1907	W. A. Larned	Robert LeRoy
1908	W. A. Larned	B. C. Wright
1909	W. A. Larned	W. J. Clothier
1910	W. A. Larned	T. C. Bundy
1911	W. A. Larned	M. E. McLoughlin
1912	M. E. McLoughlin	W. J. Johnson
1913	M. E. McLoughlin	R. N. Williams
1914	R. N. Williams	M. E. McLoughlin
1915	Wm. M. Johnston	M. E. McLoughlin
1916	R. N. Williams	Wm. M. Johnston
1917	R. L. Murray	N. W. Niles
1918	R. L. Murray	Wm. T. Tilden

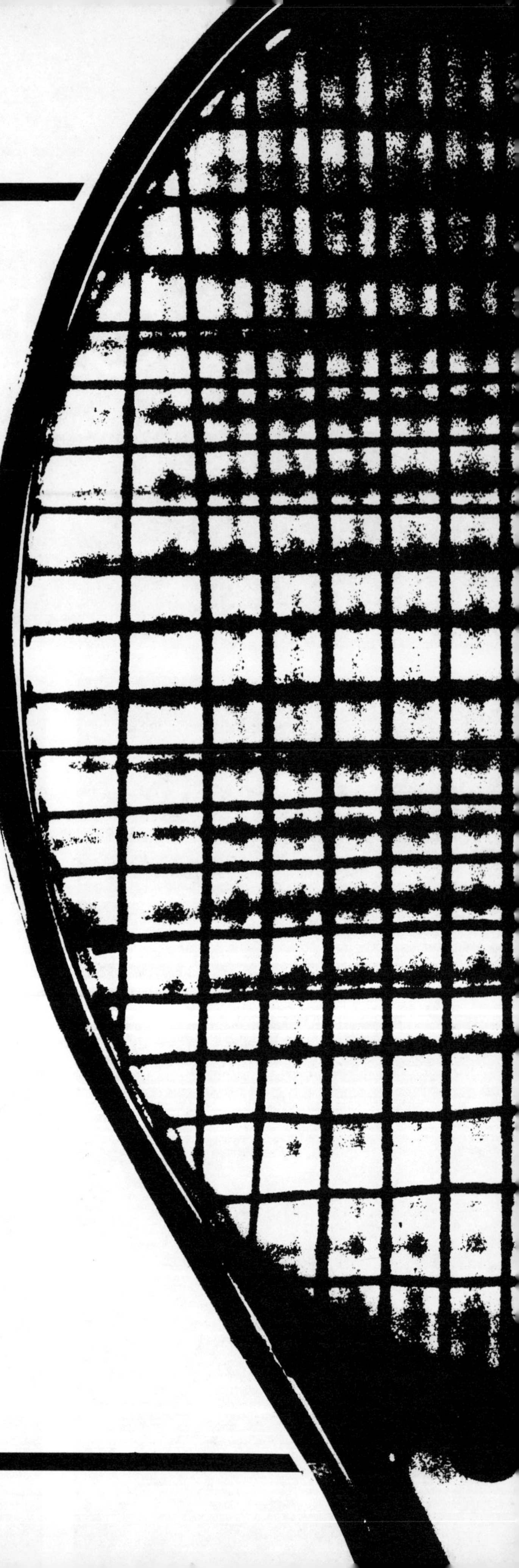

Year	Champion	Runner-up
1919	Wm. M. Johnston	Wm. T. Tilden
1920	Wm. T. Tilden	Wm. M. Johnston
1921	Wm. T. Tilden	Wallace J. Johnson
1922	Wm. T. Tilden	Wm. M. Johnston
1923	Wm. T. Tilden	Wm. M. Johnston
1924	Wm. T. Tilden	Wm. M. Johnston
1925	Wm. T. Tilden	Wm. M. Johnston
1926	Rene Lacoste	Jean Borotra
1927	Rene Lacoste	Wm. T. Tilden
1928	Henri Cochet	Francis T. Hunter
1929	Wm. T. Tilden	Francis T. Hunter
1930	John H. Doeg	Francis X. Shields
1931	H. Ellsworth Vines	George M. Lott, Jr.
1932	H. Ellsworth Vines	Henri Cochet
1933	Frederick J. Perry	John H. Crawford
1934	Frederick J. Perry	Wilmer L. Allison
1935	Wilmer L. Allison	Sidney B. Wood
1936	Frederick J. Perry	J. Donald Budge
1937	J. Donald Budge	Baron G. von Cramm
1938	J. Donald Budge	C. Gene Mako
1939	Robert L. Riggs	S. Welby Van Horn
1940	Donald McNeill	Robert L. Riggs
1941	Robert L. Riggs	Francis Kovacs 2nd
1942	Fred R. Schroeder, Jr.	Frank Parker
1943	Lt. Joseph Hunt	Seaman John Kramer
1944	Sgt. Frank A. Parker	William F. Talbert
1945	Sgt. Frank A. Parker	William F. Talbert
1946	John A. Kramer	Tom Brown, Jr.
1947	John A. Kramer	Frank A. Parker
1948	Richard A. Gonzales	Eric W. Sturgess
1949	Richard A. Gonzales	Fred R. Schroeder, Jr.
1950	Arthur Larsen	Herbert Flam
1951	Frank Sedgman	E. Victor Seixas, Jr.
1952	Frank Sedgman	Gardnar Mulloy
1953	Tony Trabert	E. Victor Seixas, Jr.
1954	E. Victor Seixas, Jr.	Rex Hartwig
1955	Tony Trabert	Ken Rosewall
1956	Ken Rosewall	Lewis Hoad
1957	Malcolm J. Anderson	Ashley J. Cooper
1958	Ashley J. Cooper	Malcolm J. Anderson
1959	Neale Fraser	Alejandro Olmedo
1960	Neale Fraser	Rodney Laver
1961	Roy Emerson	Rodney Laver
1962	Rodney Laver	Roy Emerson
1963	Rafael Osuna	Frank Froehling, III
1964	Roy Emerson	Fred Stolle
1965	Manuel Santana	Cliff Drysdale
1966	Fred Stolle	John Newcombe
1967	John Newcombe	Clark Graebner
1968	Arthur Ashe	Robert Lutz
1968	Arthur Ashe*	Tom Okker
1969	Stan Smith	Robert Lutz
1969	Rod Laver*	Tony Roche
1970	Ken Rosewall	Tony Roche
1971	Stan Smith	Jan Kodes
1972	Ilie Nastase	Arthur Ashe
1973	John Newcombe	Jan Kodes
1974	Jimmy Connors	Ken Rosewall
1975	Manuel Orantes	Jimmy Connors
1976	Jimmy Connors	Bjorn Borg
1977	Guillermo Vilas	Jimmy Connors
1978	Jimmy Connors	Bjorn Borg
1979	John McEnroe	Vitas Gerulaitis
1980	John McEnroe	Bjorn Borg

*Winner of Open championship in year when both amateur and Open tournaments were held.

USTA Women's Singles Champions

Year	Champion	Runner-up
1887	Ellen Hansell	Laura Knight
1888	Bertha Townsend	Marion Wright
1889	Bertha Townsend	Louise Voorhes
1890	Ellen C. Roosevelt	Grace Roosevelt
1891	Mabel Cahill	Elisabeth Moore
1892	Mabel Cahill	Bessie Moore
1893	Aline Terry	Mabel Cahill
1894	Helen R. Hellwig	Aline Terry
1895	Juliette Atkinson	Helen Hellwig
1896	Elisabeth Moore	Juliette Atkinson
1897	Juliette Atkinson	Bessie Moore
1898	Juliette Atkinson	Marion Jones

Year	Champion	Runner-up
1899	Marion Jones	Juliette Atkinson
1900	Myrtle McAteer	Marion Jones
1901	Elisabeth Moore	Myrtle McAteer
1902	Marion Jones	Elisabeth Moore
1903	Elisabeth Moore	Marion Jones
1904	May Sutton	Elisabeth Moore
1905	Elisabeth Moore	Helen Homans
1906	Helen Homans	Elisabeth Moore
1907	Evelyn Sears	Carrie Neely
1908	M. Barger-Wallach	Evelyn Sears
1908	Hazel Hotchkiss	M. Barger-Wallach
1910	Hazel Hotchkiss	Louise Hamond
1911	Hazel Hotchkiss	Florence Sutton
1912	Mary Browne	Elenora Sears
1913	Mary Browne	Dorothy Green
1914	Mary Browne	Marie Wagner
1915	Bella Bjurstedt	Hazel Wightman
1916	Bella Bjurstedt	Ellen Raymond
1917	Bella Bjurstedt	Marion Vanderhoef
1918	Bella Bjurstedt	Eleanore Goss
1919	Hazel Wightman	Marion Zinderstein
1920	Molla Mallory	Marion Zinderstein
1921	Molla Mallory	Mary Browne
1922	Molla Mallory	Helen Wills
1923	Helen Wills	Molla Mallory
1924	Helen Wills	Molla Mallory
1925	Helen Wills	Kathleen McKane
1926	Molla Mallory	Elizabeth Ryan
1927	Helen Wills	Betty Nuthall
1928	Helen Wills	Helen H. Jacobs
1929	Helen Wills	M. Watson
1930	Betty Nuthall	L. A. Harper
1931	Helen Wills Moody	E. B. Whittingstall
1932	Helen H. Jacobs	Caroline A. Babcock
1933	Helen H. Jacobs	Helen Wills Moody
1934	Helen H. Jacobs	Sarah H. Palfrey
1935	Helen H. Jacobs	Sarah P. Fabyan
1936	Alice Marble	Helen H. Jacobs
1937	Anita Lizane	J. Jedrzejowska
1938	Alice Marble	Nancy Wynne
1939	Alice Marble	Helen H. Jacobs
1940	Alice Marble	Helen H. Jacobs
1941	Sarah Palfrey Cooke	Pauline Betz
1942	Pauline Betz	A. Louise Brough

40

Year	Champion	Runner-up
1943	Pauline Betz	A. Louise Brough
1944	Pauline Betz	Margaret Osborne
1945	Sarah P. Cooke	Pauline Betz
1946	Pauline Betz	Patricia Canning
1947	A. Louise Brough	Margaret Osborne
1948	Margaret O. duPont	A. Louise Brough
1949	Margaret O. duPont	Doris Hart
1950	Margaret O. duPont	Doris Hart
1951	Maureen Connolly	Shirley Fry
1952	Maureen Connolly	Doris Hart
1953	Maureen Connolly	Doris Hart
1954	Doris Hart	A. Louise Brough
1955	Doris Hart	Patricia Ward
1956	Shirley J. Fry	Althea Gibson
1957	Althea Gibson	A. Louise Brough
1958	Althea Gibson	Darlene Hard
1959	Maria Bueno	Christine Truman
1960	Darlene R. Hard	Maria Bueno
1961	Darlene R. Hard	Ann Haydon
1962	Margaret Smith	Darlene Hard
1963	Maria Bueno	Margaret Smith
1964	Maria Bueno	Carole C. Graebner
1965	Margaret Smith	Billie Jean Moffitt
1966	Maria Bueno	Nancy Richey
1967	Billie Jean King	Ann Jaydon Jones
1968	Margaret S. Court	Maria Bueno
1968	Virginia Wade*	Billie Jean King
1969	Margaret S. Court	Virginia Wade
1969	Margaret S. Court*	Nancy Richey
1970	Margaret S. Court	Rosemary Casals
1971	Billie Jean King	Rosemary Casals
1972	Billie Jean King	Kerry Melville
1973	Margaret S. Court	Evonne Goolagong
1974	Billie Jean King	Evonne Goolagong
1975	Chris Evert	Evonne Goolagong
1976	Chris Evert	Evonne Goolagong
1977	Chris Evert	Wendy Turnbull
1978	Chris Evert	Pam Shriver
1979	Tracy Austin	Chris Evert Lloyd
1980	Chris Evert Lloyd	Hana Mandlikova

*Winner of Open championship in year when both amateur and Open tournaments were held.

USTA Men's Doubles Champions

Year	Champion
1881	C. M. Clark and F. W. Taylor
1882	R. D. Sears and J. Dwight
1883	R. D. Sears and J. Dwight
1884	R. D. Sears and J. Dwight
1885	R. D. Sears and J. S. Clark
1886	R. D. Sears and J. Dwight
1887	R. D. Sears and J. Dwight
1888	O. S. Campbell and V. G. Hall
1889	H. W. Slocum, Jr. and H. A. Taylor
1890	V. G. Hall and C. Hobart
1891	O. S. Campbell and Robert Huntington, Jr.
1892	O. S. Campbell and Robert Huntington, Jr.
1893	Clarence Hobart and Fred H. Hovey
1894	Clarence Hobart and Fred H. Hovey
1895	M. G. Chace and R. D. Wrenn
1896	Carr B. Neel and Samuel R. Neel
1897	Leo E. Ware and George P. Sheldon, Jr.
1898	Leo E. Ware and George P. Sheldon, Jr.
1899	Holcombe Ward and Dwight F. Davis
1900	Holcombe Ward and Dwight F. Davis
1901	Holcombe Ward and Dwight F. Davis
1902	Reginald F. Doherty and Hugh L. Doherty
1903	Reginald F. Doherty and Hugh L. Doherty
1904	Holcombe Ward and Beals C. Wright
1905	Holcombe Ward and Beals C. Wright
1906	Holcombe Ward and Beals C. Wright
1907	Fred B. Alexander and Harold H. Hackett
1908	Fred B. Alexander and Harold H. Hackett
1909	Fred B. Alexander and Harold H. Hackett
1910	Fred B. Alexander and Harold H. Hackett
1911	Raymond D. Little and Gustave Touchard
1912	Maurice McLoughlin and Thomas Bundy
1913	Maurice McLoughlin and Thomas Bundy
1914	Maurice McLoughlin and Thomas Bundy
1915	William Johnston and Clarence Griffin
1916	William Johnston and Clarence Griffin
1917	Fred Alexander and Harold Throckmorton
1918	William T. Tilden and Vincent Richards
1919	Norman E. Brookes and Gerald Patterson

Year	Champion
1920	William Johnston and Clarence Griffin
1921	William T. Tilden and Vincent Richards
1922	William T. Tilden and Vincent Richards
1923	William T. Tilden and Brian I. C. Norton
1924	Howard Kinsey and Robert Kinsey
1925	R. N. Williams, 2nd and Vincent Richards
1926	R. N. Williams, 2nd and Vincent Richards
1927	William T. Tilden and Francis T. Hunter
1928	George M. Lott, Jr. and John Hennessey
1929	George M. Lott, Jr. and John H. Doeg
1930	George M. Lott, Jr. and John H. Doeg
1931	Wilmer Allison and John Van Ryn
1932	H. Ellsworth Vines, Jr and Keith Gledhill
1933	George M. Lott, Jr. and Lester R. Stoefen
1934	George M. Lott, Jr. and Lester R. Stoefen
1935	Wilmer L. Allison and John Van Ryn
1936	J. Donald Budge and C. Gene Mako
1937	Gottfried von Cramm and Henner Henkel
1938	J. Donald Budge and C. Gene Mako
1939	Adrian K. Quist and John E. Bromwich
1940	John A. Kramer and Fred R. Schroeder, Jr.
1941	John A. Kramer and Fred R. Schroeder, Jr.
1942	Lt. Gardnar Mulloy and William Talbert
1943	John A. Kramer and Frank A. Parker
1944	W. Donald McNeill and Robert Falkenburg
1945	Lt. Gardnar Mulloy and William Talbert
1946	Gardnar Mulloy and William Talbert
1947	John A. Kramer and Fred R. Schroeder, Jr.
1948	Gardnar Mulloy and William Talbert
1949	John Bromwich and William Sidwell
1950	John Bromwich and Fred Sedgman
1951	Kenneth McGregor and Frank Sedgman
1952	Mervyn Rose and E. Victor Seixas, Jr.
1953	Rex Hartwig and Mervyn Rose
1954	E. Victor Seixas, Jr. and Tony Trabert
1955	Kosei Kamo and Atushi Miyagi
1956	Lewis Hoad and Kenneth Rosewall
1957	Ashley J. Cooper and Neale Fraser
1958	Alex Olmedo and Hamilton Richardson
1959	Neale Fraser and Roy Emerson
1960	Neale Fraser and Roy Emerson
1961	Charles McKinley and Dennis Ralston
1962	Rafael Osuna and Antonio Palafox
1963	Charles McKinley and Dennis Ralston

Year	Champion
1964	Charles McKinley and Dennis Ralston
1965	Roy Emerson and Fred Stolle
1966	Roy Emerson and Fred Stolle
1967	John Newcombe and Tony Roche
1968	Robert Lutz and Stan Smith
1968	Robert Lutz and Stan Smith*
1969	Richard Crealy and Allan Stone
1969	Ken Rosewall and Fred Stolle*
1970	Pierre Barthes and Nicki Pilic
1971	John Newcombe and Roger Taylor
1972	Cliff Drysdale and Roger Taylor
1973	Owen Davidson and John Newcombe
1974	Robert Lutz and Stan Smith
1975	Jimmy Connors and Ilie Nastase
1976	Marty Riessen and Tom Okker
1977	Bob Hewitt and Frew McMcMillan
1978	Robert Lutz and Stan Smith
1979	John McEnroe and Peter Fleming
1980	Stan Smith and Robert Lutz

*Winner of Open championship in year when both amateur and Open tournaments were held.

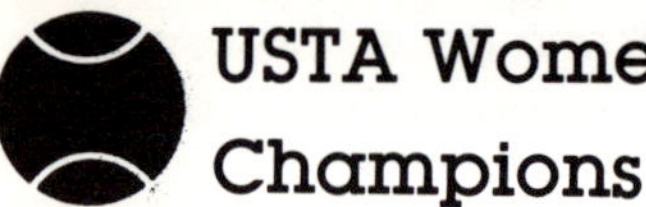

USTA Women's Doubles Champions

Year	Champion
1890	Ellen C. Roosevelt and Grace W. Roosevelt
1891	Mabel E. Cahill and Mrs. W. F. Morgan
1892	Mabel E. Cahill and A. M. McKinlay
1893	Aline M. Terry and Hattie Butler
1894	Helen R. Hellwig and Juliette P. Atkinson
1895	Helen R. Hellwig and Juliette P. Atkinson
1896	Elizabeth H. Moore and Juliette P. Atkinson
1897	Juliette P. Atkinson and Kathleen Atkinson
1898	Juliette P. Atkinson and Kathleen Atkinson
1899	Jane W. Craven and Myrtle McAteer
1900	Edith Parker and Hallie Champlin
1901	Juliette P. Atkinson and Myrtle McAteer

Year	Champion
1902	Juliette P. Atkinson and Marion Jones
1903	Elizabeth H. Moore and Carrie B. Neely
1904	May G. Sutton and Miriam Hall
1905	Helen Homans and Carrie B. Neely
1906	Mrs. L. S. Coe and Mrs. D. S. Platt
1907	Marie Weimer and Carrie B. Neely
1908	Evelyn Sears and Margaret Curtis
1909	Hazel V. Hotchkiss and Edith E. Rotch
1910	Hazel V. Hotchkiss and Edith E. Rotch
1911	Hazel V. Hotchkiss and Elenora Sears
1912	Dorothy Green and Mary K. Browne
1913	Mary K. Browne and Mrs. R. H. Williams
1914	Mary K. Browne and Mrs. R. H. Williams
1915	Hazel H. Wightman and Eleanora Sears
1916	Molla Bjurstedt and Eleanora Sears
1917	Molla Bjurstedt and Eleanora Sears
1918	Marion Zinderstein and Eleanor Goss
1919	Marion Zinderstein and Eleanor Goss
1920	Marion Zinderstein and Eleanor Goss
1921	Mary K. Browne and Mrs. R. H. Williams
1922	Marion Z. Jessup and Helen N. Wills
1923	Kathleen McKane and Phyllis H. Covell
1924	Hazel H. Wightman and Helen N. Wills
1925	Mary K. Browne and Helen N. Wills
1926	Elizabeth Ryan and Eleanor Goss
1927	Kathleen Godfree and Ermyntrude Harvey
1928	Hazel H. Wightman and Helen N. Wills
1929	Phoebe Watson and Peggy Michell
1930	Betty Nuthall and Sarah Palfrey
1931	Betty Nuthall and Eileen Whitingstall
1932	Helen Jacobs and Sarah Palfrey
1933	Betty Nuthall and Freda James
1934	Helen Jacobs and Sarah Palfrey
1935	Helen Jacobs and Sarah Palfrey Fabyan
1936	Marjorie Van Ryn and Carolin Babcock
1937	Sarah Fabyan and Alice Marble
1938	Sarah Fabyan and Alice Marble
1939	Sarah Fabyan and Alice Marble
1940	Sarah Fabyan and Alice Marble
1941	Sarah Fabyan and Margaret E. Osborne
1942	A. Louise Brough and Margaret Osborne
1943	A. Louise Brough and Margaret Osborne
1944	A. Louise Brough and Margaret Osborne
1945	A. Louise Brough and Margaret Osborne

Year	Champion
1946	A. Louise Brough and Margaret Osborne
1947	A. Louise Brough and Margaret Osborne
1948	A. Louise Brough and Margaret duPont
1949	A. Louise Brough and Margaret duPont
1950	A. Louise Brough and Margaret duPont
1951	Shirley Fry and Doris Hart
1952	Shirley Fry and Doris Hart
1953	Shirley Fry and Doris Hart
1954	Shirley Fry and Doris Hart
1955	A. Louise Brough and Margaret duPont
1956	A. Louise Brough and Margaret duPont
1957	A. Louise Brough and Margaret duPont
1958	Jeanne M. Arth and Darlene R. Hard
1959	Jeanne M. Arth and Darlene R. Hard
1960	Maria Bueno and Darlene R. Hard
1961	Darlene R. Hard and Lesley Turner
1962	Darlene R. Hard and Maria Bueno
1963	Robyn Ebbern and Margaret Smith
1964	Billie Jean Moffitt and Karen H. Susman
1965	Carole Graebner and Nancy Richey
1966	Maria Bueno and Nancy Richey
1967	Rosemary Casals and Billie Jean King
1968	Maria Bueno and Margaret Court
1969	Maria Bueno and Margaret Court*
1969	Margaret Court and Virginia Wade
1969	Francoise Durr and Darlene Hard*
1970	Margaret Court and Judy Dalton
1971	Rosemary Casals and Judy Dalton
1972	Francoise Durr and Betty Stove
1973	Margaret Court and Virginia Wade
1974	Rosemary Casals and Billie Jean King
1975	Margaret Court and Virginia Wade
1976	Delina Boshoff and Illana Kloss
1977	Martina Navratilova and Betty Stove
1978	Martina Navratilova and Billie Jean King
1979	Betty Stove and Wendy Turnbull
1980	Billie Jean King and Martina Navratilova

*Winner of Open championship in year when both amateur and Open tournaments were held.

USTA Mixed Doubles Champions

Year	Champion
1892	Mabel E. Cahill and Clarence Hobart
1893	Ellen C. Roosevelt and Clarence Hobart
1894	Juliette P. Atkinson and Edwin P. Fischer
1895	Juliette P. Atkinson and Edwin P. Fischer
1896	Juliette P. Atkinson and Edwin P. Fischer
1897	Laura Henson and D. L. Magruder
1898	Carrie B. Neely and Edwin P. Fischer
1899	Elizabeth J. Rastall and Albert L. Hoskins
1900	Margaret Hunnewell and Alfred Codman
1901	Marion Jones and Raymond D. Little
1902	Elizabeth H. Moore and Wylie C. Grant
1903	Helen Chapman and Harry F. Allen
1904	Elizabeth H. Moore and Wylie C. Grant
1905	Mr. and Mrs. Clarence Hobart
1906	Sarah Coffin and Edward B. Dewhurst
1907	May Sayres and Wallace F. Johnson
1908	Edith E. Rotch and Nathaniel W. Niles
1909	Hazel V. Hotchkiss and Wallace F. Johnson
1910	Hazel V. Hotchkiss and J. R. Carpenter, Jr.
1911	Hazel V. Hotchkiss and Wallace F. Johnson
1912	Mary K. Browne and R. N. Williams, 2nd
1913	Mary K. Browne and William T. Tilden, 2nd
1914	Mary K. Browne and William T. Tilden, 2nd
1915	Hazel H. Wightman and Harry C. Johnson
1916	Eleonora Sears and Willis F. Davis
1917	Molla Bjurstedt and Irving C. Wright
1918	Hazel H. Wightman and Irving C. Wright
1919	Marion Zinderstein and Vincent Richards
1920	Hazel H. Wightman and W. F. Johnson
1921	Mary K. Browne and William Johnston
1922	Molla B. Mallory and William T. Tilden, 2nd
1923	Molla B. Mallory and William T. Tilden, 2nd
1924	Helen N. Wills and Vincent Richards
1925	Kathleen McKane and John B. Hawkes
1926	Elizabeth Ryan and Jean Borotra
1927	Eileen Bennett and Henri Cochet
1928	Helen N. Wills and John B. Hawkes
1929	Betty Nuthall and George M. Lott, Jr.

Year	Champion
1930	Edith Cross and Wilmer L. Allison
1931	Betty Nuthall and George M. Lott, Jr.
1932	Sarah Palfrey and Frederick Perry
1933	Elizabeth Ryan and H. Ellsworth Vines, Jr.
1934	Helen H. Jacobs and George M. Lott, Jr.
1935	Sarah Palfrey Fabyan and Enrique Maier
1936	Alice Marble and C. Gene Mako
1937	Sarah P. Fabyan and J. Donald Budge
1938	Alice Marble and J. Donald Budge
1939	Alice Marble and Harry C. Hopman
1940	Alice Marble and Robert L. Riggs
1941	Sarah Palfrey Cooke and John A. Kramer
1942	A. Louise Brough and F. R. Schroeder, Jr.
1943	Margaret Osborne and William F. Talbert
1944	Margaret Osborne and William F. Talbert
1945	Margaret Osborne and William F. Talbert
1946	Margaret Osborne and William F. Talbert
1947	A. Louise Brough and John Bromwich
1948	A. Louise Brough and Thomas Brown, Jr.
1949	A. Louise Brough and Eric Sturgess
1950	Margaret O. duPont and Kenneth McGregor
1951	Doris Hart and Frank Sedgman
1952	Doris Hart and Frank Sedgman
1953	Doris Hart and E. Victor Seixas, Jr.
1954	Doris Hart and E. Victor Seixas, Jr.
1955	Doris Hart and E. Victor Seixas, Jr.
1956	Margaret O. duPont and Kenneth Rosewall
1957	Althea Gibson and Kurt Neilsen
1958	Margaret O. duPont and Neale Fraser
1959	Margaret O. duPont and Neale Fraser
1960	Margaret O. duPont and Neale Fraser
1961	Margaret Smith and Robert Mark
1962	Margaret Smith and Fred Stolle
1963	Margaret Smith and Ken Fletcher
1964	Margaret Smith and John Newcombe
1965	Margaret Smith and Fred Stolle
1966	Donna Floyd Fales and Owen Davidson
1967	Billie Jean King and Owen Davidson
1968	Mary Ann Eisel and Peter Curtis
1969	Patti Hogan and Paul Sullivan
1969	Margaret S. Court and Martin Riessen*
1970	Margaret S. Court and Martin Riessen
1971	Billie Jean King and Owen Davidson
1972	Margaret S. Court and Martin Riessen
1973	Billie Jean King and Owen Davidson
1974	Pam Teeguarden and Geoff Masters
1975	Rosemary Casals and Richard Stockton
1976	Billie Jean King and Phil Dent
1977	Betty Stove and Frew McMillan
1978	Betty Stove and Frew McMillan
1979	Bob Hewitt and Greer Stevens
1980	Wendy Turnbull and Martin Riessen

*Winner of Open championship in year when both amateur and Open tournaments were held.

ALL-ENGLAND (WIMBLEDON) CHAMPIONS

All-England (Wimbledon) Men's Singles Champions

Year	Champion	Runner-up
1877	Spencer W. Gore	W. C. Marshall
1878	P. F. Hadow	Spencer W. Gore
1879	J. T. Hartley	V. "St. Leger" Gould
1880	J. T. Hartley	H. F. Lawford
1881	William Renshaw	J. T. Hartley
1882	William Renshaw	Ernest Renshaw
1883	William Renshaw	Ernest Renshaw
1884	William Renshaw	H. F. Lawford
1885	William Renshaw	H. F. Lawford
1886	William Renshaw	H. F. Lawford
1887	H. F. Lawford	Ernest Renshaw
1888	Ernest Renshaw	H. F. Lawford
1889	William Renshaw	Ernest Renshaw
1890	W. J. Hamilton	William Renshaw
1891	Wilfred Baddeley	Joshua Pim
1892	Wilfred Baddeley	Joshua Pim
1893	Joshua Pim	Wilfred Baddeley
1894	Joshua Pim	Wilfred Baddeley
1895	Wilfred Baddeley	Wilberforce V. Eaves
1896	H. S. Mahoney	Wilfred Baddeley
1897	Reggie F. Doherty	H. S. Mahoney
1898	Reggie F. Doherty	H. Laurie Doherty
1899	Reggie F. Doherty	Arthur W. Gore
1900	Reggie F. Doherty	Sidney H. Smith
1901	Arthur W. Gore	Reggie F. Doherty
1902	H. Laurie Doherty	Arthur W. Gore
1903	H. Laurie Doherty	Frank L. Riseley
1904	H. Laurie Doherty	Frank L. Riseley
1905	H. Laurie Doherty	Norman E. Brookes
1906	H. Laurie Doherty	Frank L. Riseley
1907	Norman E. Brookes	Arthur W. Gore
1908	Arthur W. Gore	H. Roper Barrett
1909	Arthur W. Gore	M. G. J. Ritchie
1910	Anthony F. Wilding	Arthur W. Gore
1911	Anthony F. Wilding	H. Roper Barrett
1912	Anthony F. Wilding	Arthur W. Gore
1913	Anthony F. Wilding	M. E. McLoughlin
1914	Norman E. Brookes	Anthony F. Wilding
1915-18	not held	
1919	Gerald L. Patterson	Norman E. Brookes
1920	William T. Tilden II	Gerald L. Patterson
1921	William T. Tilden II	Brian I. C. Norton
1922	Gerald L. Patterson	Randolph Lycett
1923	William M. Johnston	Francis T. Hunter
1924	Jean Borotra	Jean Rene Lacoste
1925	Jean Rene Lacoste	Jean Borotra
1926	Jean Borotra	Howard Kinsey
1927	Henri Cochet	Jean Borotra
1928	Jean Rene Lacoste	Henri Cochet
1929	Henri Cochet	Jean Borotra
1930	William T. Tilden II	Wilmer Allison
1931	Sidney Wood	Frank X. Shields
1932	Ellsworth Vines	Wilfred Austin
1933	Jack Crawford	Ellsworth Vines
1934	Fred J. Perry	Jack Crawford
1935	Fred J. Perry	Gottfried von Cramm
1936	Fred J. Perry	Gottfried von Cramm
1937	J. Donald Budge	Gottfried von Cramm
1938	J. Donald Budge	Wilfred Austin
1939	Robert L. Riggs	Elwood Cooke
1940-45	not held	
1946	Yvon Petra	Geoff E. Brown
1947	Jack Kramer	Tom P. Brown
1948	Bob Falkenburg	John Bromwich
1949	Fred R. Schroeder, Jr.	Jaroslav Drobny
1950	Budge Patty	Frank Sedgman
1951	Dick Savitt	Ken McGregor
1952	Frank Sedgman	Jaroslav Drobny
1953	E. Victor Seixas, Jr.	Kurt Nielsen
1954	Jaroslav Drobny	Ken Rosewall
1955	Tony Trabert	Kurt Nielsen
1956	Lew Hoad	Ken Rosewall
1957	Lew Hoad	Ashley Cooper
1958	Ashley Cooper	Neale Fraser
1959	Alex Olmedo	Rod Laver
1960	Neale Fraser	Rod Laver
1961	Rod Laver	Chuck McKinley
1962	Rod Laver	Martin Mulligan
1963	Chuck McKinley	Fred Stolle
1964	Roy Emerson	Fred Stolle
1965	Roy Emerson	Fred Stolle

Year	Champion	Runner-up
1966	Manuel Santana	Dennis Ralston
1967	John Newcombe	Wilhelm Bungert
1968	Rod Laver	Tony Roche
1969	Rod Laver	John Newcombe
1970	John Newcombe	Ken Rosewall
1971	John Newcombe	Stan Smith
1972	Stan Smith	Ilie Nastase
1973	Jan Kodes	Alex Metreveli
1974	Jimmy Connors	Ken Rosewall
1975	Arthur Ashe	Jimmy Connors
1976	Bjorn Borg	Ilie Nastase
1977	Bjorn Borg	Jimmy Connors
1978	Bjorn Borg	Jimmy Connors
1979	Bjorn Borg	Roscoe Tanner
1980	Bjorn Borg	John McEnroe

All-England (Wimbledon) Women's Singles Champions

Year	Champion	Runner-up
1884	Maud Watson	Lillian Watson
1885	Maud Watson	Blanche Bingley
1886	Blanche Bingley	Maud Watson
1887	Lottie Dod	Blanche Bingley
1888	Lottie Dod	Blanche B. Hillyard
1889	Blanche B. Hillyard	L. Rice
1890	L. Rice	L. Jacks
1891	Lottie Dod	Blanche B. Hillyard
1892	Lottie Dod	Blanche B. Hillyard
1893	Lottie Dod	Blanche B. Hillyard
1894	Blanche B. Hillyard	L. Austin
1895	Charlotte Cooper	H. Jackson
1896	Charlotte Cooper	Mrs. W. H. Pickering
1897	Blanche B. Hillyard	Charlotte Cooper
1898	Charlotte Cooper	L. Martin
1899	Blanche B. Hillyard	Charlotte Cooper
1900	Blanche B. Hillyard	Charlotte Cooper
1901	Charlotte C. Sterry	Blanche B. Hillyard
1902	M. E. Robb	Charlotte C. Sterry
1903	Dorothea Douglas	E. W. Thompson
1904	Dorothea Douglas	Charlotte C. Sterry
1905	May Sutton	Dorothea Douglas
1906	Dorothea Douglas	May Sutton
1907	May Sutton	Dorothea Chambers
1908	Charlotte C. Sterry	A. M. Morton
1909	Dora Boothby	A. M. Morton
1910	Dorothea Chambers	Dora Boothby
1911	Dorothea Chambers	Dora Boothby
1912	E. W. T. Larcombe	Charlotte C. Sterry
1913	Dorothea Chambers	Mrs. R. J. McNair
1914	Dorothea Chambers	E. W. T. Larcombe
1915-18	not held	
1919	Suzanne Lenglen	Dorothea Chambers
1920	Suzanne Lenglen	Dorothea Chambers
1921	Suzanne Lenglen	Elizabeth Ryan
1922	Suzanne Lenglen	Molla Mallory
1923	Suzanne Lenglen	Kitty McKane
1924	Kitty McKane	Helen Wills
1925	Suzanne Lenglen	Joan Fry
1926	Kitty M. Godfree	Lili Alvarez
1927	Helen Wills	Lili Alvarez
1928	Helen Wills	Lili Alvarez
1929	Helen Wills	Helen Jacobs
1930	Helen W. Moody	Elizabeth Ryan
1931	Cilly Aussem	Hilda Krahwinkel
1932	Helen W. Moody	Helen Jacobs
1933	Helen W. Moody	Dorothy Round
1934	Dorothy Round	Helen Jacobs
1935	Helen W. Moody	Helen Jacobs
1936	Helen Jacobs	Hilda K. Sperling
1937	Dorothy Round	J. Jedrzejowska
1938	Helen W. Moody	Helen Jacobs
1939	Alice Marble	Kay Stammers
1940-45	not held	
1946	Pauline Betz	A. Louise Brough
1947	Margaret Osborne	Doris Hart
1948	A. Louise Brough	Doris Hart
1949	A. Louise Brough	Margaret O. duPont

Year	Champion	Runner-up
1950	A. Louise Brough	Margaret O. duPont
1951	Doris Hart	Shirley Fry
1952	Maureen Connolly	A. Louise Brough
1953	Maureen Connolly	Doris Hart
1954	Maureen Connolly	A. Louise Brough
1955	A. Louise Brough	Beverly Baker Fleitz
1956	Shirley Fry	Angela Buxton
1957	Althea Gibson	Darlene Hard
1958	Althea Gibson	Angela Mortimer
1959	Maria Bueno	Darlene Hard
1960	Maria Bueno	Sandra Reynolds
1961	Angela Mortimer	Christine Truman
1962	Karen H. Susman	Vera P. Sukova
1963	Margaret Smith	Billie Jean Moffitt
1964	Maria Bueno	Margaret Smith
1965	Margaret Smith	Maria Bueno
1966	Billie Jean King	Maria Bueno
1967	Billie Jean King	Maria Bueno
1968	Billie Jean King	Judy Tegart
1969	Ann Haydon Jones	Billie Jean King
1970	Margaret S. Court	Billie Jean King
1971	Evonne Goolagong	Margaret S. Court
1972	Billie Jean King	Evonne Goolagong
1973	Billie Jean King	Chris Evert
1974	Chris Evert	Olga Morozova
1975	Billie Jean King	Evonne Goolagong
1976	Chris Evert	Evonne G. Cawley
1977	Virginia Wade	Betty Stove
1978	Martina Navratilova	Chris Evert
1979	Martina Navratilova	Chris Evert Lloyd
1980	Evonne G. Cawley	Chris Evert Lloyd

All-England (Wimbledon) Men's Doubles Champions

Year	Champion
1879	L. R. Erskine and H. F. Lawford
1880	William and Ernest Renshaw
1881	William and Ernest Renshaw
1882	J. T. Hartley and R. T. Richardson
1883	C. W. Grinstead and C. E. Welldon
1884	William and Ernest Renshaw
1885	William and Ernest Renshaw
1886	William and Ernest Renshaw
1887	Herbert W. Wilberforce and P. B. Lyon
1888	William and Ernest Renshaw
1889	William and Ernest Renshaw
1890	Joshua Pim and F. O. Stoker
1891	Wilfred and Herbert Baddeley
1892	E. W. Lewis and H. S. Barlow
1893	Joshua Pim and F. O. Stoker
1894	Wilfred and Herbert Baddeley
1895	Wilfred and Herbert Baddeley
1896	Wilfred and Herbert Baddeley
1897	Reggie F. and H. Laurie Doherty
1898	Reggie F. and H. Laurie Doherty
1899	Reggie F. and H. Laurie Doherty
1900	Reggie F. and H. Laurie Doherty
1901	Reggie F. and H. Laurie Doherty
1902	Sidney H. Smith and Frank Riseley
1903	Reggie F. and H. Laurie Doherty
1904	Reggie F. and H. Laurie Doherty
1905	Reggie F. and H. Laurie Doherty
1906	Sidney H. Smith and Frank Riseley
1907	Norman Brookes and Anthony Wilding
1908	Anthony Wilding and M. G. J. Ritchie
1909	Arthur W. Gore and H. R. Barrett
1910	Anthony Wilding and M. G. J. Ritchie
1911	Andre Gobert and Max Decugis
1912	H. R. Barrett and Charles Dixon
1913	H. R. Barrett and Charles Dixon
1914	Norman Brookes and Anthony Wilding
1915-18	not held

Year	Champion
1919	R. V. Thomas and Pat O'Hara Wood
1920	R. N. Williams and C. S. Garland
1921	Randolph Lycett and Max Woosnam
1922	J. O. Anderson and Randolph Lycett
1923	Leslie A. Godfree and Randolph Lycett
1924	Frank Hunter and Vincent Richards
1925	Jean Borotra and Jean Rene Lacoste
1926	Jacques Brugnon and Henri Cochet
1927	Frank Hunter and William Tilden II
1928	Jacques Brugnon and Henri Cochet
1929	Wilmer Allison and John Van Ryn
1930	Wilmer Allison and John Van Ryn
1931	George M. Lott and John Van Ryn
1932	Jean Borotra and Jacques Brugnon
1933	Jean Borotra and Jacques Brugnon
1934	George M. Lott and Lester R. Stoefen
1935	Jack Crawford and Adrian Quist
1936	G. Pat Hughes and Raymond Tuckey
1937	Don Budge and Gene Mako
1938	Don Budge and Gene Mako
1939	Ellwood Cooke and Robert L. Riggs
1940-45	not held
1946	Tom Brown and John Kramer
1947	Robert Falkenburg and John Kramer
1948	John Bromwich and Frank Sedgman
1949	Richard Gonzales and Frank Parker
1950	John Bromwich and Adrian Quist
1951	Ken McGregor and Frank Sedgman
1952	Ken McGregor and Frank Sedgman
1953	Lew Hoad and Ken Rosewall
1954	Rex Hartwig and Mervyn Rose
1955	Rex Hartwig and Lew Hoad
1956	Lew Hoad and Ken Rosewall
1957	Budge Patty and Gardnar Mulloy
1958	Sven Davidson and Ulf Schmidt
1959	Roy Emerson and Neale Fraser
1960	Rafael Osuna and Dennis Ralston
1961	Roy Emerson and Neale Fraser
1962	Bob Hewitt and Fred Stolle
1963	Rafael Osuna and Antonio Palafox
1964	Bob Hewitt and Fred Stolle
1965	John Newcombe and Tony Roche
1966	Ken Fletcher and John Newcombe
1967	Bob Hewitt and Frew McMillan

Year	Champion
1968	John Newcombe and Tony Roche
1969	John Newcombe and Tony Roche
1970	John Newcombe and Tony Roche
1971	Roy Emerson and Rod Laver
1972	Bob Hewitt and Frew McMillan
1973	Jimmy Connors and Ilie Nastase
1974	John Newcombe and Tony Roche
1975	Vitras Gerulaitis and Alex Mayer
1976	Brian Gottfried and Raoul Ramirez
1977	Ross Case and Geoff Masters
1978	Bob Hewitt and Frew McMillan
1979	John McEnroe and Peter Fleming
1980	Peter McNamara and Paul McNamee

All-England (Wimbledon) Women's Doubles Champions

Year	Champion
1913	Mrs. R. J. McNair and Dora Boothby
1914	A. M. Morton and Elizabeth Ryan
1915-18	not held
1919	Suzanne Lenglen and Elizabeth Ryan
1920	Suzanne Lenglen and Elizabeth Ryan
1921	Suzanne Lenglen and Elizabeth Ryan
1922	Suzanne Lenglen and Elizabeth Ryan
1923	Suzanne Lenglen and Elizabeth Ryan
1924	Hazel Wightman and Helen Wills
1925	Suzanne Lenglen and Elizabeth Ryan
1926	Mary K. Browne and Elizabeth Ryan
1927	Helen Wills and Elizabeth Ryan
1928	Peggy Saunders and Phyllis Watson
1929	Peggy Michell and Phyllis Watson
1930	Helen Wills Moody and Elizabeth Ryan
1931	Phyllis Mudford and Dorothy S. Barron

Year	Champion
1932	Doris Metaxa and Josane Sigart
1933	Simone Mathieu and Elizabeth Ryan
1934	Simone Mathieu and Elizabeth Ryan
1935	Freda James and Kay Stammers
1936	Freda James and Kay Stammers
1937	Simone Mathieu and Billie Yorke
1938	Sarah Palfrey Fabyan and Alice Marble
1939	Sarah Palfrey Fabyan and Alice Marble
1940-45	not held
1946	A. Louise Brough and Margaret Osborne
1947	Pat Todd and Doris Hart
1948	A. Louise Brough and Margaret O. duPont
1949	A. Louise Brough and Margaret O. duPont
1950	A. Louise Brough and Margaret O. duPont
1951	Doris Hart and Shirley Fry
1952	Doris Hart and Shirley Fry
1953	Doris Hart and Shirley Fry
1954	A. Louise Brough and Margaret O. DuPont
1955	Angela Mortimer and Anne Shilcock
1956	Angela Buxton and Althea Gibson
1957	Althea Gibson and Darlene Hard
1958	Maria Bueno and Althea Gibson
1959	Jean Arth and Darlene Hard
1960	Maria Bueno and Darlene Hard
1961	Karen Hantze and Billie Jean Moffitt
1962	Billie Jean Moffitt and Karen H. Susman
1963	Maria Bueno and Darlene Hard
1964	Margaret Smith and Lesley Turner
1965	Marie Bueno and Billie Jean Moffitt
1966	Maria Bueno and Nancy Richey
1967	Rosemary Casals and Billie Jean King
1968	Rosemary Casals and Billie Jean King
1969	Margaret Smith Court and Judy Tegart
1970	Rosemary Casals and Billie Jean King
1971	Rosemary Casals and Billie Jean King
1972	Billie Jean King and Betty Stove
1973	Billie Jean King and Rosemary Casals
1974	Evonne Goolagong and Peggy Michel
1975	Ann Kiyomura and Kazuko Sawamatsu
1976	Chris Evert and Martina Navratilova
1977	Helen Gourlay Cawley and JoAnn Russell
1978	Wendy Turnbull and Kerry M. Reid
1979	Billie Jean King and Martina Navratilova
1980	Kathy Jordan and Anne Smith

All-England (Wimbledon) Mixed Doubles Champions

Year	Champion
1913	J. Hope Crispe and Mrs. C. O. Tuckey
1914	J. C. Parke and E. W. Thomson Larcombe
1915-18	not held
1919	Randolph Lycett and Elizabeth Ryan
1920	Gerald Patterson and Suzanne Lenglen
1921	Randolph Lycett and Elizabeth Ryan
1922	Pat O'Hara Wood and Suzanne Lenglen
1923	Randolph Lycett and Elizabeth Ryan
1924	J. Brian Gilbert and Kitty McKane
1925	Jean Borotra and Suzanne Lenglen
1926	Leslie Godfree and Kitty McKane Godfree
1927	Francis T. Hunter and Helen Wills
1928	Pat Spence and Elizabeth Ryan
1929	Francis T. Hunter and Helen Wills
1930	Jack Crawford and Elizabeth Ryan
1931	George M. Lott and Mrs. L. A. Harper
1932	Enrique Majer and Elizabeth Ryan
1933	Gottfried von Cramm and Hilda Krahwinkel
1934	Ryuki Mike and Dorothy Round
1935	Fred J. Perry and Dorothy Round
1936	Fred J. Perry and Dorothy Round
1937	Don Budge and Alice Marble
1938	Don Budge and Alice Marble
1939	Robert L. Riggs and Alice Marble
1940-45	not held
1946	Tom Brown and A. Louise Brough
1947	John Bromwich and A. Louise Brough
1948	John Bromwich and A. Louise Brough
1949	Eric Sturgess and Sheila Summers
1950	Eric Sturgess and A. Louise Brough
1951	Frank Sedgman and Doris Hart
1952	Frank Sedgman and Doris Hart
1953	E. Victor Seixas and Doris Hart
1954	E. Victor Seixas and Doris Hart
1955	E. Victor Seixas and Doris Hart
1956	E. Victor Seixas and Shirley Fry
1957	Mervyn Rose and Darlene Hard

Year	Champion
1958	Bob Howe and Loraine Coghlan
1959	Rod Laver and Darlene Hard
1960	Rod Laver and Darlene Hard
1961	Fred Stolle and Lesley Turner
1962	Neale Fraser and Margaret O. duPont
1963	Ken Fletcher and Margaret Smith
1964	Fred Stolle and Lesley Turner
1965	Ken Fletcher and Margaret Smith
1966	Ken Fletcher and Margaret Smith
1967	Owen Davidson and Billie Jean King
1968	Ken Fletcher and Margaret Smith Court
1969	Fred Stolle and Ann Jones
1970	Ilie Nastase and Rosemary Casals
1971	Owen Davidson and Billie Jean King
1972	Ilie Nastase and Rosemary Casals
1973	Owen Davidson and Billie Jean King
1974	Owen Davidson and Billie Jean King
1975	Marty Riessen and Margaret Smith Court
1976	Tony Roche and Francoise Durr
1977	Bob Hewitt and Greer Stevens
1978	Frew McMillan and Betty Stove
1979	Bob Hewitt and Greer Stevens
1980	John Austin and Tracy Austin

RACQUET SIZES

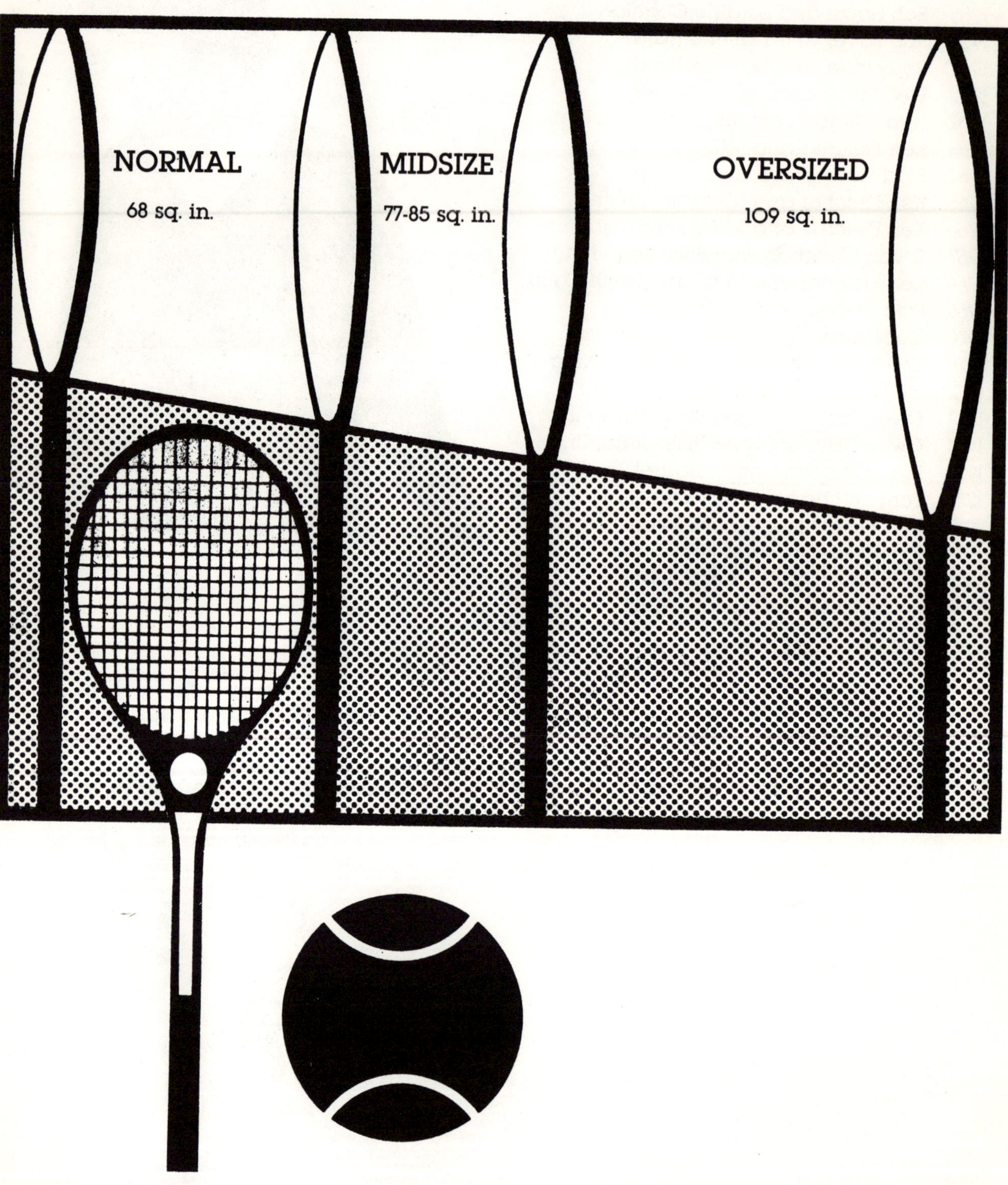

USTA RANKINGS

USTA MEN'S RANKINGS

1970

1. Cliff Richey
2. Stan Smith
3. Arthur Ashe
4. Clark Graebner
5. Bob Lutz
6. Tom Gorman
7. Jim Osborne
8. Jim McManus
9. Barry MacKay
10. Charles Pasarell

1971

1. Stan Smith
2. Cliff Richey
3. Clark Graebner
4. Tom Gorman
5. Jimmy Connors
6. Erik van Dillen
7. F. A. Froehling III
8. Roscoe Tanner
9. Alex Olmedo
10. Harold Solomon

1972

1. Stan Smith
2. Tom Gorman
3. Jimmy Connors
4. Dick Stockton
5. Roscoe Tanner
6. Harold Solomon
7. Erik van Dillen
8. Clark Graebner
9. Pancho Gonzalez
10. Brian Gottfried

1973

1. Jimmy Connors
   and Stan Smith
3. Arthur Ashe
4. Tom Gorman
5. Cliff Richey
6. Charles Pasarell
7. Marty Riessen
8. Erik van Dillen
9. Brian Gottfried
10. Bob Lutz

1974

1. Jimmy Connors
2. Stan Smith
3. Marty Riessen
4. Roscoe Tanner
5. Arthur Ashe
6. Tom Gorman
7. Dick Stockton
8. Harold Solomon
9. Charles Pasarell
10. Jeff Borowiak

1975

1. Arthur Ashe
2. Jimmy Connors
3. Roscoe Tanner
4. Vitas Gerulaitis
5. Eddie Dibbs
6. Brian Gottfried
7. Harold Solomon
8. Bob Lutz
9. Cliff Richey
10. Dick Stockton

1976

1. Jimmy Connors
2. Eddie Dibbs
3. Arthur Ashe
4. Harold Solomon
5. Brian Gottfried
6. Roscoe Tanner
7. Dick Stockton
8. Stan Smith
9. Vitas Gerulaitis
10. Bob Lutz

1977

1. Jimmy Connors
2. Brian Gottfried
3. Vitas Gerulaitis
4. Eddie Dibbs
5. Dick Stockton
6. Harold Solomon
7. Stan Smith
8. Roscoe Tanner
9. Bob Lutz
10. John McEnroe

1978

1. Jimmy Connors
2. Vitas Gerulaitis
3. Brian Gottfried
4. Eddie Dibbs
5. John McEnroe
6. Gene Mayer
7. Roscoe Tanner
8. Harold Solomon
9. Arthur Ashe
10. Dick Stockton

1979

1. John McEnroe
2. Jimmy Connors
3. Roscoe Tanner
4. Vitas Gerulaitis
5. Arthur Ashe
6. Eddie Dibbs
7. Harold Solomon
8. Peter Fleming
9. Gene Mayer
10. Brian Gottfried

USTA WOMEN'S RANKINGS

1970

1. Billie Jean M. King
2. Rosemary Casals
3. Nancy Richey Gunter
4. Mary Ann E. Curtis
5. Patti St. Ann Hogan
6. Jane Bartkowicz
7. Valerie Jean Ziegenfuss
8. Kristie Sue Pigeon
9. Stephanie Johnson
10. Denise Carter Triolo

1971

1. Billie Jean King
2. Rosemary Casals
3. Chris Evert
4. Nancy Richey Gunter
5. Mary Ann Eisel
6. Julie Heldman
7. Jane Bartkowicz
8. Linda Tuero
9. Patti St. Ann Hogan
10. Denise Carter Triolo

1972

1. Billie Jean King
2. Nancy Richey Gunter
3. Chris Evert
4. Rosemary Casals
5. Wendy Overton
6. Patti Hogan
7. Linda Tuero
8. Julie M. Heldman
9. Pam Teegarden
10. Janet Newberry

1973

1. Billie Jean King
2. Chris Evert
3. Rosemary Casals
4. Nancy Richey Gunter
5. Julie M. Heldman
6. Pam Teegarden
7. Kristien Kemmer
8. Janet Newberry
9. Valerie Ziegenfuss
10. Wendy Overton

1974

1. Chris Evert
2. Billie Jean King
3. Rosemary Casals
4. Nancy Richey Gunter
5. Julie M. Heldman
6. Kathy Kuykendall
7. Pam Teegarden
8. Valerie Ziegenfuss
9. Jeanne Evert
10. Marcelyn Louie

1975

1. Chris Evert
2. Nancy Richey Gunter
3. Julie M. Heldman
4. Wendy Overton
5. Marcelyn Louie
6. Mona Schallau
7. Kathy Kuykendall
8. Janet Newberry
9. Terry Holladay
10. Rosemary Casals

1976

1. Chris Evert
2. Rosemary Casals
3. Nancy Richey Gunter
4. Terry Holladay
5. Marita Redondo
6. Mona S. Guerrant
7. Kathy May
8. JoAnne Russell
9. Janet Newberry
10. Kathy Kuykendall

1977

1. Chris Evert
2. Billie Jean King
3. Rosemary Casals
4. Tracy Austin
5. JoAnne Russell
6. Kathy May
7. Terry Holladay
8. Kristien K. Shaw
9. Janet Newberry
10. Laura DuPont

1978

1. Chris Evert
2. Billie Jean King
3. Tracy Austin
4. Rosemary Casals
5. Pam Shriver
6. Marita Redondo
7. Kathy May
8. Ann Smith
9. JoAnne Russell
10. Jeanne DuVall

1979

1. Martina Navratilova
2. Chris Evert Lloyd
3. Tracy Austin
4. Billie Jean King
5. Kathy Jordan
6. Ann Kiyomura
7. Caroline Stoll
8. Kathy May Teacher
9. Kate Latham
10. Terry Holladay

DEFENSIVE VOLLEY

ANNUAL PRIZE-MONEY LIST

MEN'S PRIZE MONEY LIST

1970

1.	Rod Laver	$201,453
2.	Arthur Ashe	141,018
3.	Ken Rosewall	140,455
4.	Cliff Richey	97,000
5.	Roy Emerson	96,485
6.	Stan Smith	95,251
7.	John Newcombe	78,251
8.	Pancho Gonzalez	77,365
9.	Clark Graebner	68,000
10.	Tony Roche	67,232

1971

1.	Rod Laver	$292,717
2.	Ken Rosewall	138,317
3.	Tom Okker	120,465
4.	Ilie Nastase	114,000
5.	Arthur Ashe	104,642
6.	Stan Smith	103,806
7.	John Newcombe	101,514
8.	Marty Riessen	87,310
9.	Clark Graebner	75,400
10.	Cliff Richey	75,000

1972

1.	Ilie Nastase	$176,000
2.	Stan Smith	142,300
3.	Ken Rosewall	132,950
4.	John Newcombe	120,600
5.	Arthur Ashe	119,775
6.	Rod Laver	100,200
7.	Tom Okker	90,004
8.	Jimmy Connors	90,000
9.	Marty Riessen	74,436
10.	Cliff Drysdale	68,433

1973

1.	Ilie Nastase	$228,750
2.	Stan Smith	218,647
3.	Tom Okker	178,215
4.	Jimmy Connors	156,400
5.	John Newcombe	151,675
6.	Arthur Ashe	141,206
7.	Rod Laver	140,325
8.	Ken Rosewall	120,420
9.	Manuel Orantes	97,175
10.	Brian Gottfried	87,710

1974

1.	Jimmy Connors	$281,309
2.	Guillermo Vilas	274,327
3.	John Newcombe	273,299
4.	Bjorn Borg	215,229
5.	Ilie Nastase	190,752
6.	Arthur Ashe	165,194
7.	Stan Smith	163,326
8.	Manuel Orantes	139,857
9.	Rod Laver	134,600
10.	Paul Ramirez	127,425

1975

1.	Jimmy Connors	$600,273
2.	Arthur Ashe	338,337
3.	Manuel Orantes	271,066
4.	Guillermo Vilas	247,372
5.	Bjorn Borg	229,875
6.	Raul Ramirez	210,850
7.	Ilie Nastase	210,793
8.	Brian Gottfried	171,130
9.	Rod Laver	165,321
10.	John Alexander	158,650

1976

1.	Jimmy Connors	$687,335
2.	Ilie Nastase	576,705
3.	Raul Ramirez	465,942
4.	Bjorn Borg	424,420
5.	Arthur Ashe	373,886
6.	Manuel Orantes	361,884
7.	Harold Solomon	253,432
8.	Guillermo Vilas	250,726
9.	Eddie Dibbs	239,821
10.	Vojtek Fibak	234,039

1977

1.	Jimmy Connors	$922,657
2.	Guillermo Vilas	800,642
3.	Bjorn Borg	480,661
4.	Brian Gottfried	478,988
5.	Dick Stockton	311,856
6.	Ilie Nastase	306,956
7.	Vitas Gerulaitis	294,324
8.	Eddie Dibbs	283,691
9.	Roscoe Tanner	281,131
10.	Raul Ramirez	245,007

1978

1.	Eddie Dibbs	$582,872
2.	Raul Ramirez	450,110
3.	John McEnroe	445,024
4.	Wojteck Fibak	383,843
5.	Ilie Nastase	367,422
6.	Vitas Gerulaitis	359,095
7.	Harold Solomon	354,732
8.	Jimmy Connors	353,307
9.	Bjorn Borg	348,386
10.	Brian Gottfried	312,205

1979

1.	Bjorn Borg	$1,019,345
2.	John McEnroe	1,005,238
3.	Jimmy Connors	701,340
4.	Vitas Gerulaitis	414,515
5.	Guillermo Vilas	373,195
6.	Peter Fleming	353,315
7.	Roscoe Tanner	263,433
8.	Eddie Dibbs	249,293
9.	Wojtek Fibak	234,452
10.	Harold Solomon	222,078

WOMEN'S PRIZE MONEY LIST

1971

1.	Billie Jean King	$117,000
2.	Francoise Durr	65,000
3.	Rosemary Casals	62,000
4.	Judy Dalton	33,867
5.	Kerry Melville	29,767
6.	Ann Haydon	26,148
7.	Virginia Wade	24,000
8.	Nancy R. Gunter	15,300
9.	Mary Ann Eisel	15,000
10.	Valerie Ziegenfuss	14,000

1972

1.	Billie Jean King	$119,000
2.	Rosemary Casals	70,000
3.	Kerry Melville	55,000
4.	Nancy R. Gunter	50,800
5.	Margaret S. Court	47,000
6.	Francoise Durr	46,000
7.	Evonne Goolagong	42,000
8.	Virginia Wade	32,800
9.	Wendy Overton	30,000
10.	Karen Krantzcke	19,312

1973

1.	Margaret S. Court	$204,400
2.	Billie Jean King	194,700
3.	Chris Evert	152,002
4.	Evonne Goolagong	108,127
5.	Rosemary Casals	105,375
6.	Kerry Melville	61,200
7.	Virginia Wade	60,100
8.	Nancy R. Gunter	48,292
9.	Francoise Durr	40,727
10.	Betty Stove	40,049

1974

1.	Chris Evert	$261,460
2.	Billie Jean King	173,225
3.	Evonne Goolagong	102,506
4.	Virginia Wade	85,389
5.	Rosemary Casals	72,389
6.	Julie Heldman	60,511
7.	Kerry Melville	56,022
8.	Francoise Durr	41,227
9.	Olga Morozova	40,927
10.	Betty Stove	40,249

1975

1.	Chris Evert	$412,977
2.	Martina Navratilova	185,518
3.	Virginia Wade	153,576
4.	Evonne Goolagong	145,254
5.	Billie Jean King	124,900
6.	Margaret S. Court	105,646

1976

1.	Chris Evert	$343,165
2.	Evonne Goolagong	209,952
3.	Virginia Wade	159,213
4.	Rosemary Casals	128,685
5.	Martina Navratilova	128,535
6.	Betty Stove	98,358

1977

1.	Chris Evert	$503,134
2.	Martina Navratilova	300,317
3.	Virginia Wade	258,746
4.	Betty Stove	229,162
5.	Billie Jean King	193,194
6.	Sue Barker	190,498
7.	Kerry Reid	156,234
8.	Rosemary Casals	126,193
9.	Dianne Fromholtz	106,410
10.	Wendy Turnbull	98,568

1978

1.	Martina Navratilova	$450,757
2.	Chris Evert	354,486
3.	Virginia Wade	270,027
4.	Kerry Reid	208,766
5.	Wendy Turnbull	189,583
6.	Betty Stove	177,243
7.	Evonne Goolagong	160,844
8.	Virginia Ruzici	151,379
9.	Billie Jean King	149,492
10.	Regina Marsikova	88,894

1979

1.	Martina Navratilova	$747,548
2.	Chris Evert Lloyd	564,398
3.	Tracy Austin	541,676
4.	Wendy Turnbull	317,463
5.	Dianne Fromholtz	265,990
6.	Billie Jean King	185,804
7.	Betty Stove	182,006
8.	Sue Barker	175,452
9.	Evonne Goolagong	171,573
10.	Virginia Wade	146,283

Photo by Russ Adams

GREAT MATCHES

A match between two great tennis players is perhaps the most exciting contest in all of sport. Tennis is not like golf, where each contestant struggles against par. Nor is it like track, where the clock is the adversary. Tennis is head-to-head competition in a confined area with play continuing until one competitor overcomes the other.

Other ingredients work to intensify the excitement. The players involved, their temperament, character, and the ranking of each. Bjorn Borg and John McEnroe, Evonne Goolagong and Chris Evert, each evoke a different set of emotional responses from the spectator.

The setting, whether Wimbledon or Forest Hills, Longwood or Newport, plays a role. The stakes have to be considered. Some matches have historic overtones, altering the course of tennis history.

No one can really say which matches of the past should be stamped the most exciting and significant of all time. But the pages that follow mention a few that should be considered.

BUDGE VON CRAMM

Forest Hills 1937

Don Budge, born in California in 1917, succeeded Fred Perry and Bill Tilden as the greatest player of the day. Tall, lean, and red-haired, Budge first gained national acclaim at the age of eighteen when he faced England's Fred Perry, world champion at the time. In a spirited battle, Budge managed to extend Perry to five sets before losing.

Budge's power shots awed the spectators. His lightning backhand was a killer stroke. He also had a searing service and a ruthless overhead smash. He was said to have a weakness on the forehand side, but it was a failing that opponents seldom managed to exploit.

Late in 1937 when he arrived at Forest Hills for the American championships, Budge could look back on a triumphant season. He had won at Wimbledon, claiming not only the singles title, but the doubles and mixed doubles championships as well. Time and again, he had beaten the best players of France, England, Germany, Australia, and his own country. Yet he had not won a U.S. championship.

Budge breezed through the early rounds at Forest Hills, winning his matches by lopsided scores. In the finals, he faced one of the aristocrats of lawn tennis, Baron Gottfried von Cramm of Germany. Known for a superior forehand and flawless court manners, von Cramm had won the French championship in 1934 and 1936, but a major victory had eluded him. For three consecutive years beginning in 1935, he had lost in the finals at Wimbledon.

The appeal of Budge, a young American on the brink of greatness, and the drama of his match against the elegant German, set turnstiles clicking as they had not in years. On the day of the final match, every seat in the stadium of the West Side Tennis Club was filled, and that had only happened twice before in the history of the championships. The best tickets which normally sold for $2.75, were being scalped for as much as $8.

Budge wasted no time in taking command. Hitting the full-length of the court on one stroke after another, he got his opponent on the run, and then kept him running. Von Cramm's forehand betrayed him on one stroke after another and his backhand volleys were faulty. The set went to Budge, 6-1.

Budge's backers displayed confident grins. But not for long. As the second set began, the courtly von Cramm fought back furiously, slashing hard drives from every part of the court and taking the net at the slightest opportunity. With the huge crowd cheering him on, von Cramm surged to a 3-1 lead. Budge managed to regain control and even won three points in a row, edging ahead, 4-3, but in the end the revivified von Cramm prevailed, 9-7.

Budge's supporters now wore worried frowns. Von Cramm's thunderous serves and forehands, combined with his willingness to take the net and volley, were making the Californian a defensive player. But their frowns melted as the third set began. Budge took over the attack, unleashing all of his weapons. The fury of Budge's assault forced von Cramm to commit countless errors and the set was over quickly, Budge winning, 6-1.

Now the question was whether von Cramm could fight back as he had done earlier. The set began serenely, but then von Cramm caught fire. Budge found himself unable to cope with von Cramm's drives that kicked high to his backhand, and when he sought to take the net the baron inevitably passed him with a backhand straight down the line. The set went to von Cramm.

As the final set began, the two men fought on even terms—but only briefly. At 1-1, Budge moved ahead with an overpowering backhand drive. It seemed to signal what was ahead for von

Cramm. Although he fought valiantly to stem the tide, Budge took the last five games of the set, with the loss of only seven points to his opponent. When a backhand volley off of Budge's racket brought the match to a close, a thunderous cheer went up from the stands.

For the next two years, Budge was the pre-eminent figure in world tennis. He became the first man to hold the four big championships, Australia, France, England, and America, a feat he accomplished in 1938. He compiled an awesome 25-4 won-lost record in Davis Cup play. He became the first tennis player to win the distinguished Sullivan Trophy. But more than a few observers say that he was never better than he was in the fifth set against Gottfried von Cramm at Forest Hills in 1937.

GONAZALES SCHROEDER

Forest Hills 1949

In 1948, the U.S. champion was Richard (Pancho) Gonzales, a big man with a big game. Besides his power, Gonzales could play with a delicate touch. Born in Los Angeles in 1928, the first of seven children, Gonzales grew up with a mania for tennis. He had no professional coaching, he was entirely self-taught. Yet in 1943 at the age of fifteen, he was ranked No. 1 in his age group in southern California. After a stretch in the Navy, he won the southern California championship and was ranked No. 17 nationally. Only sixteen months later, in September 1948, he won the singles crown at Forest Hills.

When Gonzales sought to retain his title in 1949, he faced Californian Frederick R. (Ted) Schroeder, who had previously won the American singles title in 1942. In the intervening years, Schroeder had not bothered to play at Forest Hills, preferring to remain in California and sell refrigerators.

The stadium was filled to overflowing as the match got underway. The first set was one of the most memorable ever played at Forest Hills, Schroeder winning, 18-16. The record-breaking 34 games spanned one hour and thirteen minutes.

In the thirtieth game, the set was almost decided in Gonzales' favor. Schroeder was trailing, O-4O, when Gonzales lifted a perfect lob over his head. But Schroeder managed to retrieve the ball and win the point. The crowd watched tensely, ready to rock the stadium with cheers. Another faultless lob by Gonzales was successfully returned by the challenger, who then pulled out of the seemingly hopeless situation with a pair of service aces and a smoking overhead smash.

Gonzales refused to become discouraged and won the next service. Schroeder, playing with magnificent patience, broke through in the thirty-third game, but not as he might have wished. During a rapid exchange of strokes, Gonzales executed a deft drop volley. "Out!" cried the side linesman. Whistles and catcalls erupted from the stands. Gonzales started to protest, too, then decided to accept the decision.

In the next rally, the last of the set, Gonzales strode forward and reached out to volley—and slipped. The ball plopped into the net. The crowd gasped.

To have lost the set after fighting for so long, as long as many matches last, was enough to break the spirit of any player. In the next set, Gonzales appeared to be a beaten champion, losing docilely, 6-2.

But by the third set, Gonzales had thrown off his dejection and began demonstrating to his fans that he did not plan to surrender. His serve started booming again, his footwork speeded up, and his volleys became crisp and accurate. He took four games in a row without deuce once being called and captured the set with relative ease.

The ten minute rest period did little to restore any potency to Schroeder's game. The champion broke the challenger in the very first game and went on from that point to even the match. Now everything rode on the one final set.

Schroeder had a history of performing tenaciously in clutch situations, and now he added to his reputation. He took the first game after being down 0-30, and then threatened to break Gonzales in the fourth game. But a backhand attempt to pass when an easy volley went astray, and Gonzales drew even again.

In the ninth game, Gonzales broke Schroeder with a blistering backhand return. For the first time, the champion was ahead. Schroeder stood quietly, a bit shocked, a bit disbelieving. Gonzales kissed his racket and went out to serve for the match.

Every point in the final game brought loud cheers or groans from the stands. When Gonzales double-faulted to make the score 15-all, they groaned. When he fell behind, 30-40, they groaned again.

Schroeder returned service and Gonzales, who had raced in behind his serve, volleyed to force an error. Now it was deuce.

Gonzales got the advantage with an overhand smash that dented the turf. The stands rang with cries of joy. In the final frantic rally, Schroeder raced far to his left, and whipped a backhand past Gonzales at the net. The crowd gasped. Then all hell broke loose as the linesman signaled it was out.

Schroeder, rushing back to his normal playing position, was stunned by the call. "Out?" he cried. Then he broke into a grin, pretended to throw his racket at the official, and ran to the net to congratulate Gonazles. Everyone was standing and cheering.

Years later, Gonzales, attending a tennis luncheon in New York, was asked whether he remembered the last shot. "I'll never forget it," he said. "It missed the line by a mile."

Schroeder was also asked about the shot. "All through the years, I've always believed it was good," he said. "I still say that. Of course, you can mesmerize yourself into believing anything. Each time I think about it, the ball comes closer to center court."

KING ● SMITH

Wimbledon 1966

There are zipper-like scars across her kneecaps now and she's told the world more than once that she's not going to play Wimbledon or any other of the "big ones" any more. But Billy Jean King always recants those statements. She's made more comebacks than "I Love Lucy."

Why do it after all those triumphs, all that money? Why jeopardize your position, your reputation? "I play because I love it," she says. "I don't have to play; I never did. Nobody makes you play."

"I think it's mostly a striving for perfection. People think of me as being real competitive, but I think I'm more of a perfectionist. I still relate it to being as perfect as possible."

Billie Jean King's reign as the international queen of tennis began in 1966 when she won the first of her many Wimbledon championships, upsetting three-time world champion Maria Bueno in a tense, hard-fought match. But that meeting, despite its significance, did not equal the drama and excitement generated by King's semi-final match against Australia's Margaret Smith.

King had been at Wimbledon before and come very close. In 1963, at the age of twenty-one, she had lost in the finals to Margaret Smith. And just a year before, in 1965, Maria Bueno had beaten her in the finals.

In 1966, however, King would not be denied, even though in Margaret Smith she faced a woman marvelously equipped to play tennis. Big-boned and well-muscled, she stood 5-foot-10 and weighed 155. She combined speed and power with such precision that she seemed at times to be the equal of the male stars of the day.

"She simply overpowers her opponents," King said of her rival. "You have to get on top of her at the start and never let her get away. If she breaks on top her confidence soars and she is murderous."

King was determined not to let this happen. Knowing that the Australian liked to take the net and volley, King mixed drop returns with artful lobs and kept the champion off balance. Smith helped King take an early lead by serving two double faults in the second game.

In the earlier rounds of the tournament, King had been guilty of misplayed ground strokes and careless volleys. But now she played faultless and brilliant tennis, whipping one winner after another. The set went to King, 6-3.

Smith started the second set more positively, more aggressively, and built a 3-0 lead. But in the fifth game, King went on the attack again, delivering a series of exceptional backhand returns that enabled her to break Smith's serve and get back into the match.

At 3-3 she broke Smith's serve again to edge ahead. The eighth game was critical. Smith battled her way to game point and a chance to rebreak King and even the match. Then King slammed a ball that carried deep into the court. Smith thought it was out, but a linesman called it good. The decision upset Smith, and when King applied pressure, she folded. At 5-3, King executed several magnificent volleys to take the set and match, judged by many observers to be the finest victory of her career.

In the final against Maria Bueno, King faced a tense, taut, inhibited rival who failed to play the tennis of which she was capable. King, on the other hand, played confidently, sending her serves wide to Bueno's forehand, which opened up the backhand court for her first volley. Her soft drops and feathery lobs, the same weapons she had used against Smith, had the same effect, keeping Bueno reeling.

After taking the first set, 6-3, King suffered a letdown, and the set went to Bueno. In the final set, King took control of the matters early and broke Bueno in the fourth game. From that point, she surged to a 6-1 victory.

So began Billie Jean King's incredible string of victories in major tournaments. She won the Wimbledon singles crown again the next year, and also in 1968, 1972, 1973, and 1975. She won the U.S. Open in 1967, 1971, 1972, and 1974.

"All I can do is train my brains out, and eat right, and think right," King said not long after her victory at Wimbledon in 1975. "When I go out and play tennis, I'm like a little kid. I know what it is to win. I know what it is to lose. I know I don't have much time left, and I'm going to make the most of it."

ASHE OKKER

Forest Hills 1968

The year 1968 is significant in tennis history for it marked the beginning of open tennis. For the first time, Wimbledon, Forest Hills, and other traditional tournaments accepted the entries of not only amateurs but also professionals. Open tennis helped to trigger the tennis boom which lasted for years.

Before the advent of open tennis, the men's amateur tennis schedule consisted of about fifteen worthwhile events a year, with the players receiving money under the table. Professional tennis was made up of several different tours, the members journeying hither and yon with hardly anyone paying any attention to them. Nowadays, of course, there is at least one tournament of significance each week, and some weeks there are several going on at the same time in different continents.

In the first U.S. Open at Forest Hills, 25-year-old Arthur Ashe defeated Tom Okker in five sets, 14-12, 5-7, 6-3, 3-6, 6-3. It was a popular victory. Ashe had first emerged as a tennis star as a boy growing up in Richmond, Virginia. Since he was not permitted to play in that city's tournament because he was black, Ashe transferred to an integrated high school in St. Louis. There he won the U.S. interscholastic championships and the U.S. indoor championships. He went on to the University of California on a tennis scholarship. He played at Forest Hills in 1965 and got as far as the semifinals. After two years in the Army, he returned to the tennis wars, winning the Madison Square Garden Challenge Tennis Cup and the U.S. Amateur Championship at Longwood.

Some observers found Ashe's brand of tennis exciting; others didn't. Because he had the ability to hit the ball harder and faster than anyone else, he often blasted it right by his opponents. The sheer velocity of his strokes could awe the spectators. But because many of his points were over in the blink of an eye, Ashe's brand of tennis also caused some yawns.

Ashe did not look like a power hitter. He stood 6-foot-1; he weighed 155. "Wispy" and "gangly" were words often used to describe him. His enormous power came from his marvelous coordination.

Tom Okker, Ashe's rival in the final match, was a slim, speedy Dutchman. Okker had played some of the best tennis of his career in the months just before Forest Hills, winning the South African and Italian championships. In the semifinals at Forest Hills, he knocked out Australia's Ken Rosewall.

Ashe and Okker had battled for more than two hours as the fifth and deciding set began, with Okker starting to show the effects of the long struggle. In the second game, his serve lost its sting, and Ashe's powerful returns propelled him to a 40-30 lead. And when he angled a forehand that Okker could not retrieve, Ashe had his service break. Now all he had to do was hold his serve four times to win.

But at 4-2, Ashe ran into difficulty. On his second serve at 30-all, he sent the ball to Okker's backhand. The Dutchman ran around it and belted a forehand passing shot. Another point and Ashe would be broken.

But Ashe took the next point for deuce, then earned the advantage when Okker's backhand return went beyond the baseline. Okker then chipped Ashe's serve into the net. Ashe had held for 5-2. Ashe won the ninth game at love, powering an ace on the second point. It was his twenty-sixth ace of the match.

As an amateur, Ashe received only expense money for his victory. It amounted to $20 a day, a total of $280. Okker, classified as a "registered player," won $14,000. Not long after, the USLTA changed the rules of professionalism, correcting such inequities.

LAVER ROCHE

Forest Hills 1969

Don Budge registered the first Grand Slam in tennis in 1938. Australia's Rod Laver became the second man to sweep the Australian, French, British and American championships, the international events that make up the slam, in 1962. But Laver did it as an amateur. Such noteworthy professionals as Pancho Gonzales, Ken Rosewall, Lew Hoad and Tony Trabert were ineligible for the competition.

The situation changed with the advent of open tennis in 1968. The very next year, Laver became the first player in tennis history to complete a second sweep of the Big Four titles, whipping both amateurs and professionals. The 31-year-old Laver nailed down the final championship he needed by defeating fellow Australian Tony Roche, 7-9, 6-1, 6-2, 6-2, in the U.S. Open at Forest Hills.

Morning rain dampened the court, and Laver and Roche had to wait 1 hour, 35 minutes until a rented helicopter could dry the grass. "Playing conditions were difficult," Laver was to say afterwards. "The ground was very soft and you were sliding all over." Before the tenth game of the first set, Laver, trailing 4-5, switched from sneakers to spiked shoes. "They helped me considerably," Laver said, "even though I lost the first set while wearing them. But I felt good and was able to move better." Roche wore sneakers throughout the match.

Laver was behind 30-40 in the opening game of the second set, and Roche seemed on his way to breaking him and perhaps rolling a two-set lead. But three strong first serves saved the game for Laver and he won the set's last three service games at love.

Another critical moment came in the second game of the third set. Roche had held serve for a 1-0 edge when rain forced a 30-minute delay. A similar situation had occured in Laver's semifinal match with Arthur Ashe, the latter having to serve following a delay. Laver broke him immediately and went on to take the set, and, with the set that followed, the match. Although Roche managed to force Laver to deuce in their second game, Laver uncorked two big serves that bounded deep to Roche's backhand and which enabled him to hold service. He broke Roche in the next game.

"Tenniswise, winning the slam was tougher because of all the good players," Laver said after. "Pressurewise, I don't think it was any tougher. There's always pressure when you're playing for something over nine months."

BORG ● McENROE

Wimbledon 1980

"One of the most extraordinary contests in the annals of sport," Sports Illustrated called it. "Electrifying," said Fred Stolle, a former Australian great. They were referring to the Wimbledon final in 1980, with top-seeded Bjorn Borg defeating second-seeded John McEnroe. Borg did it by the amazing score of 1-6, 7-5, 6-3, 6-7, (16-18 in the tie breaker) and 8-6.

For the stolid, silent Borg, it was his thirty-fifth consecutive match victory at Wimbledon, and it gained him his fifth straight championship. "For sure, it is the best match I have ever played at Wimbledon," said the 24-year-old Borg afterward. He also said it was his toughest.

As the match got underway, McEnroe took charge, handling Borg's volley attempts with elan, turning them into points. McEnroe broke Borg the first time the Swede served, and the third time, too, scoring a quick 6-1 victory.

With his punishing serve and

go-for-broke volleys, the brash McEnroe continued to dominate play in the early stages of the second set. At 30-all, 14 of McEnroe's 41 points on serve had been won on aces, service winners, or errant returns. But later in the set, Swedish lightning struck. With McEnroe serving at 5-6, Borg ripped a backhand down the line that gave him double set point, and he was quick to wrap matters up.

Borg broke for a 2-0 lead in the third set and held for 5-2 after a 20-point game in which McEnroe had five break points. The fourth set loomed as the final one. Borg had gotten his serve-and-volley game in high gear, and his forehand and two-handed backhand were working beautifully. When Borg broke McEnroe with a brilliant backhand cross-court return at 4-all, it appeared the match was all but over, with Borg closing in on the biggest win of his life. He now only had to hold his serve.

But then—inexplicably—Borg failed to keep the pressure on his younger rival. His first serve lacked its usual fire and he began to volley tentatively. McEnroe accepted the invitation and scrambled back from double-match point to knot the match at 5-all and then send it into a tie-breaking round.

For the next 22 minutes, the pair engaged in some of the most excruciating tennis ever seen. Borg had five championship points, McEnroe seven set points. Both men served, passed, and volleyed furiously, lunging desperately and often sprawling on the scarred turf, but neither could slam the door shut. The crowd would alternately scream and then grow quiet.

McEnroe took the advantage, 17-16, when Borg's forehand service return was wide by inches. Attacking off McEnroe's next serve, Borg netted a forehand volley. McEnroe had won the set; the match was even.

"This is terrible; I'm going to lose," Borg said to himself as he took the court for the final set. "If you lose a match like this, the Wimbledon final, after all those chances, you will not forget it for a long, long time." Borg lost the first two points. "Don't get tight; don't get tight," he kept telling himself. He served the next point and won, and then kept winning, taking the game at 30, and he did not lose another point on serve until the tenth game, an incredible string of 19 consecutive points. McEnroe struggled, showing the strain of the match that had lasted almost four hours and that had followed a difficult match with Jimmy Connors the day before. He had to fight hard to hold serve from 0-40 in the second game and again for 0-40 in the eighth game.

The match ended when McEnroe, attacking a second serve, sliced a forehand volley into the corner. Borg pounced on it to counter with a backhand cross-court winner. As the crowd roared, Borg fell to his knees and clasped his hands in front of him.

As the first modernday player to win five consecutive Wimbledon championships, Borg had made tennis history. His goal, Borg has often said, is to leave the sport as the No. 1 player of all time. As far as Wimbledon is concerned, no one doubts that he has already achieved that distinction.

HALL OF FAME ENSHRINEES

HALL OF FAME ENSHRINEES

When, in 1881, representatives of American tennis clubs met in New York to standardize the playing rules, they not only performed that deed, but they were responsible for two other landmark accomplishments. They founded the United States National Lawn Tennis Association, forerunner of the USTA, and they awarded the first national championship matches to Newport. The matches remained at Newport until 1915 when the tournament was shifted to Forest Hills.

It's fitting, then, that the International Tennis Hall of Fame be located at the Newport site. Officially sanctioned by the USTA in 1954, the Hall of Fame has expanded from one room to the entire Newport Casino Building. The exhibits include a collection of tennis art, halls resplendent with ornate trophies and tennis memorabilia, and displays documenting important milestones in tennis history.

Outside the main building are the Casino's twelve carefully tended grass courts, the only grass courts in the United States open for play to the public. Another unique feature is the recently restored court-tennis court, where visitors can see the ancient "sport of kings" played as it was in Europe in the 13th century.

Each summer the Hall of Fame hosts two major tournaments. These are the last remaining professional events to be played on grass in the United States.

A second important event each summer is the ceremony on center court where newly nominated individuals are enshrined. The legendary players who have won the great events at Forest Hills and Wimbledon; at Longwood and Merion, in Sydney and Melbourne, and already achieved membership, are listed below. Presumably, reservations have been made for Ashe, Borg, McEnroe, Connors, Smith, King, Wade, Evert, Goolagong, Navratilova, Laver, Hoad, Rosewall, Emerson, and Santana.

	Year Enshrined
Pauline Betz Addie	1965
George T. Adee	1964
Fred B. Alexander	1961
Wilmer L. Allison	1963
Manuel Alonso	1977
Juliette Atkinson	1974
Lawrence A. Baker	1975
Maud Barger-Wallach	1958
Karl Behr	1969
Jean Borotra	1976
Maureen Connolly Brinker	1968
Norman Everard Brookes	1977
Mary K. Browne	1957
Jacques Brugnon	1976
J. Donald Budge	1964
Maria Bueno	1978
Mary Sutton Bundy	1956
Mabel Cahill	1976
Oliver S. Campbell	1955
Malcolm Chace	1961
Louise Brough Clapp	1967
Joseph S. Clark	1955
William J. Clothier	1956
Henri Cochet	1976
Margaret Smith Court	1979
Gottfried von Cramm	1977
John H. Crawford	1979
Allison Danzig	1968
Sarah Palfrey Danzig	1963
Dwight F. Davis	1956
John H. Doeg	1962
H. Laurence Doherty	1980
Reginald Doherty	1980
Margaret Osborne duPont	1967
Dr. James Dwight	1955
Pierre Etchebaster	1978
Robert Falkenburg	1974
Charles S. Garland	1969

	Year Enshrined
Althea Gibson	1971
Kathleen McKane Godfree	1978
Richard A. Gonzales	1968
Bryan M. Grant, Jr.	1972
Clarence Griffin	1970
Gustaf V, King of Sweden	1980
Harold H. Hackett	1961
Ellen Forde Hansell	1965
Darlene R. Hard	1973
Doris Hart	1969
Gladys Heldman	1979
Lewis Hoad	1980
Harry Hopman	1978
Fred Hovey	1974
Joseph R. Hunt	1966
Francis T. Hunter	1961
Shirley Fry Irvin	1970
Helen Hull Jacobs	1962
William Johnston	1958
Perry Jones	1970
John A. Kramer	1968
Rene Lacoste	1976
Al Laney	1979
Wiliam A. Larned	1956
Arthur D. Larsen	1969
Suzanne Lenglen	1978
George M. Lott, Jr.	1964
C. Gene Mako	1973
Molla Bjurstedt Mallory	1958
Alice Marble	1964
Alastair B. Martin	1973
Maurice McLoughlin	1957
W. Donald McNeill	1965
Elisabeth H. Moore	1971
Gardnar Mulloy	1972
R. Lindley Murray	1958
Julian S. Myrick	1963
Arthur C. Nielsen, Sr.	1971

	Year Enshrined
Rafael Osuna	1979
Frank A. Parker	1966
Budge Patty	1977
Theodore R. Pell	1967
Frederick J. Perry	1975
Vincent Richards	1961
Robert L. Riggs	1967
Helen Wills Roark	1959
Ellen C. Roosevelt	1975
Kenneth Rosewall	1980
Elizabeth Ryan	1972
Richard Savitt	1976
Frederick R. Schroeder	1966
Eleonora Sears	1968
Richard D. Sears	1955
Frank Sedgman	1979
E. Victor Seixas, Jr.	1971
Francis X. Shields	1964
Betty Nuthall Shoemaker	1977
Henry W. Slocum, Jr.	1955
William F. Talbert	1967
William T. Tilden, II	1959
Bertha Townsend Toulmin	1974
Tony Trabert	1970
James H. Van Alen	1965
John Van Ryn	1963
H. Ellsworth Vines	1962
Marie Wagner	1969
Holcombe Ward	1956
Watson Washburn	1965
Malcolm D. Whitman	1955
Hazel Hotchkiss Wightman	1957
Anthony Wilding	1978
Richard Norris Williams, 2nd	1957
Sidney B. Wood	1964
Robert D. Wrenn	1955
Beals C. Wright	1956

GLOSSARY

GLOSSARY

ace A point earned by serving a ball which cannot be returned.

ad Short for advantage.

ad court Short for advantage court.

advantage A point won by a player after deuce. Should the same player win the next point, he wins the game. If he loses the point, the score reverts to deuce.

advantage court The left-hand service court. The ball is served into the left-hand service court whenever one player or the other has the advantage.

all A term used in scoring which means "for each" or "apiece," as "30 all," referring to points in a game. "One all" refers to games.

alley The area between the service court and the sideline on the doubles court which is out of bounds in singles play.

American twist A serve in which the ball is sliced with topspin, causing it to bounce unusually high and to the receiver's left when it hits the ground.

approach A hard, deep shot, usually into one of the corners, that puts an opponent on the defensive, allowing a player to advance to the net.

Australian formation In doubles, an arrangement of the players in which the server's partner plays on the same side of the court as the server. It is normally used when the receiving player is strong in handling cross-court returns. Also called the I formation.

backcourt The part of the court farthest from the net, specifically, the area behind the service line.

backhand A stroke made with the hitting arm and racket across the body and the back of the hand facing the direction of movement.

back room The area of the court between the baseline and the fence or wall that bounds the court.

backspin Reverse spin imparted to a ball that causes it to bounce backward upon making contact with the ground.

backswing The initial movement of the arm and racket into a position for a forward or downward swing.

ball person An individual, usually a boy or girl, who retrieves balls for the players.

baseline The back line at either

end of the court.

baseline game A style of play in which a player remains on or near the baseline, playing ground strokes and seldom advancing to the net.

baseliner An individual who plays a baseline game.

break To win a game against an opponent's service. Short for service break.

bye In an elimination tournament, the position of a participant who, following the pairing of opponents, automatically advances to the next round without playing.

cannonball A hard, flat serve.

center mark A short line that bisects the baseline and indicates the edge of the area in which a player is permitted to stand when serving.

center-service line (See half-court line.)

center strap (or strop) The strip of canvas, two inches in width, down the middle of the net that is anchored to the court to hold the bottom of the net in place.

chalk The white, powdery material used to mark the lines on a court.

backhand

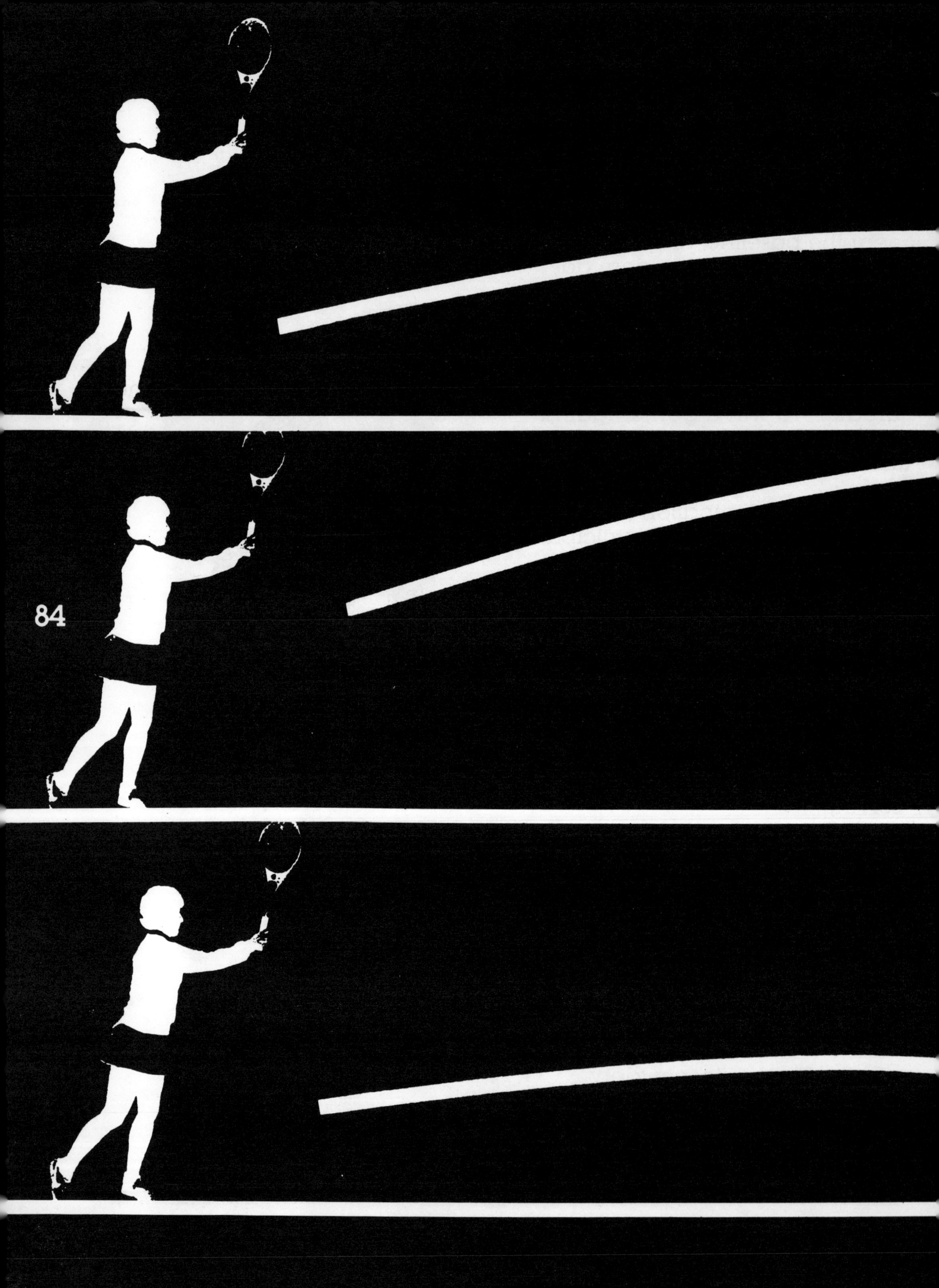

FLAT

UNDERSPIN

challenge round A match between a defending champion or titleholder and a challenger who has won an elimination tournament. The defending champion is not required to play before the challenge round and thereby cannot lose in the early stages of competition.

change-over A process, marked by a pause in the match, whereby players change to opposite sides of the net. The rules dictate a change-over must be made at the end of every odd game during a set.

chip A return made by slicing the ball, usually with backspin, and aiming at the opponent's feet.

choke To shorten one's grip on the handle of the racket, gripping more toward the head.

chop To hit the ball with a short, sharp downward stroke, imparting backspin.

consolation round A contest held for competitors who have lost in the early stages of a tournament.

continental grip A method of gripping the racket that is in between the Eastern forehand and backhand grips, with the palm near the top edge of the handle.

court The rectangular area, 78 feet long and 36 feet wide, upon which the game is played.

cross-court A stroke that sends the ball toward the diagonally opposite court.

dead A ball that is temporarily out of play and not subject to being hit, as when a ball hits the ground twice.

default The failure of a player to compete or side to compete in a scheduled match, resulting in an automatic win for the opposition.

defensive volley A volley made from below net level.

deuce A tie after each side has a score of 40; one side must score two consecutive points to win the game.

dink A soft hit that falls just beyond the net.

double fault Two successive faults while serving which result in the loss of the point.

double hit A stroke in which the ball is struck twice. A double hit is illegal and the player loses the point or serve.

doubles A form of play between two pairs of players with two players on a side.

draw The process by which players' names are drawn at random and paired on a tournament draw sheet.

drive A hard stroke or one that causes the ball to travel in a relatively flat trajectory.

drive volley A volley executed in the same manner as a forehand drive.

drop shot A soft shot that just clears the net and drops abruptly.

drop volley A drop shot made on a volley.

Eastern grip A grip in which the palm is at the side of the handle (when the face of the racket is vertical) so that the V between the thumb and forefinger is at the top of the handle.

error The failure to make a legal return.

face The flat, stringed surface of the racket.

fast A court that is hard or slick and upon which a ball has a long skid and low bounce.

fault A violation of the service rules. Two consecutive faults result in the loss of a point.

15 The first point made in a tennis game; also called 5.

flat serve A hard hit serve with little spin.

foot fault An infraction of the service rules resulting from the illegal placement of the server's feet.

forced error An error made by an opponent because of a good shot by his opponent.

forcing shot A shot that forces an opponent to be on the defensive and out of position for a subsequent shot.

forecourt The area in front of the service line.

forehand A stroke made with the palm facing the direction of movement.

40 The third point made in a tennis game. When both players reach a score of 40, it is called deuce.

gallery An area for spectators at the side or in the back of the court.

game The unit of scoring next higher than a point.

game point A situation in which the side that is leading can win the game by winning the next point.

grand slam The winning of the

four major tennis championships —the French Open, Australian Open, Wimbledon, and the U.S. Open—in one year.

ground stroke A stroke made by hitting the ball after it bounces.

hack To make a poor swing at the ball.

hacker A poor player.

half-court line The line from the net to the service line that divides the front part of each court into halves, into the right and left service courts. Also called center-service court.

half volley A stroke made just as the ball is leaving the ground.

head The principal part of the racket that makes contact with the ball.

I formation (See Australian formation).

kill shot A shot that is hit so hard that it is virtually unreturnable.

let A served ball that does not count and must be replayed. A let is called when a serve strikes the net before landing in the service court.

linesman An official whose duty it is to decide when a ball is out of bounds.

lob A stroke in which the ball is lifted high into the air over the opponent's head to land near the back of the court.

lob volley A volleying stroke hit over the head of an opponent.

love A score of zero for one side.

love game A game in which the losing player scores no points.

love set A set in which the losing player wins no games.

match Tennis competition of a specified maximum number of sets which concludes when one player wins a majority of the sets. In women's championship competition, matches are decided on the basis of two out of three sets; in men's competition, three of five sets.

match point A situation in which the player who is leading can win the match by winning the next point.

midcourt The area of the court between the net and the baseline.

mixed doubles Doubles play with each team made up of a man and a woman.

net The open-meshed fabric that divides the court in half and over which the ball must be hit.

net ball On any stroke but the serve, a ball that touches the net and continues over it to remain in play.

net game A style of play in which a player stays in the fore-court, close to the net, and volleys.

net person In doubles play, the partner who stays close to the net.

net stick The stick used to support the net at a height of 42 inches during singles play.

no man's land The area of the court between the baseline and the service line. Players standing in this area usually have difficulty playing the ball because it is frequently hit at or near their feet.

not up The call made by an official when a player just misses reaching a ball before it bounces a second time.

open A tournament or other contest in which both amateurs and professionals are eligible to compete.

overhand A stroke made with the hand brought forward and down from above shoulder level.

overhead A stroke made by hit-

OVERHEAD

ting the ball while it is in the air above the head.

overspin (See topspin.)

pass To make a passing shot against an opponent.

passing shot A hard shot driven to one side of and beyond the reach of an opponent.

poach In doubles, to hit a ball which normally would be played by one's partner. The term usually applies to play at the net.

point The smallest unit of scoring. The points have individual names—15 (or 5) for the first point; 30 for the second; 40 for the third, and, for the last, game. If both players reach 40, the situation is known as deuce. One player must then gain a lead of two points to win the game.

put away To hit a kill shot.

racket The implement used to strike or hit the ball.

rally A prolonged sequence of play in which opposing players alternately hit the ball over the net until one fails to make a good return. Also, to practice or warm up by playing the ball over the net to one's opponent.

ranking Listing players according to the level of their performances over a given period of time.

referee The official in charge of a match.

retrieve To return a difficult shot.

return To hit the ball back over the net.

round A stage in an elimination tournament in which competitors are paired and only the winners can advance to the next stage.

round robin A tournament in which every contestant meets every other contestant in turn. The final standings are determined by the overall won-lost records.

rush the net To charge to the net after making a stroke to be in the position to volley the opponent's return.

seed To schedule players in a tournament so that the superior ones will not meet in the early rounds.

serve The act of putting the ball in play by tossing it into the air and hitting it over the net into the opponent's service court.

server The player who is serving.

service The act or instance of serving.

GRIPS

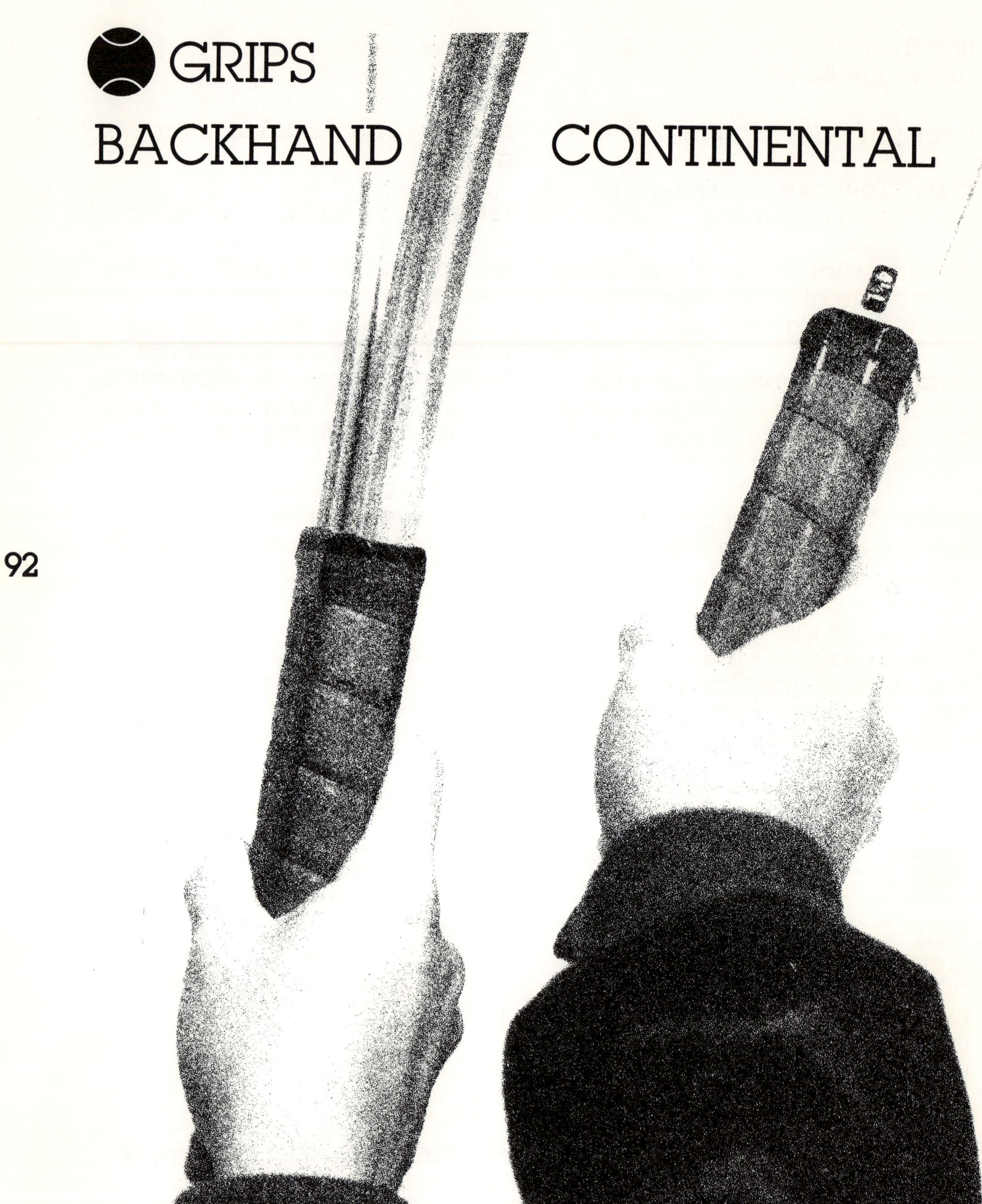

BACKHAND CONTINENTAL

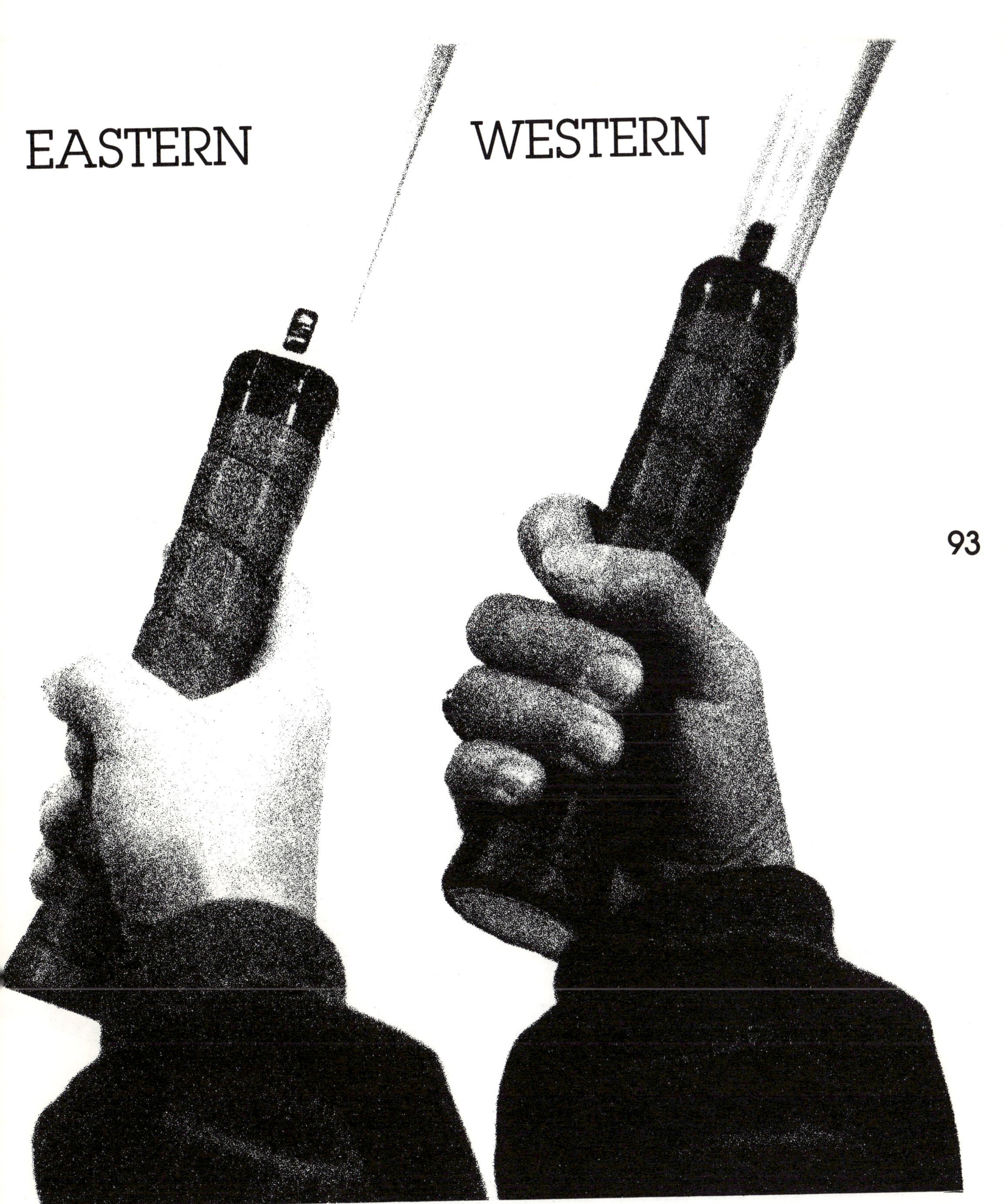
EASTERN
WESTERN

service ace An ace scored by the server.

service break The instance of a player winning a game against the opponent's serve.

service court Either of the two areas on each side of the court between the mid-court line and service sideline extending from the net back to the service line.

service line The line on each side of the court that is parallel to and 21 feet from the net that marks the rear boundary of the service court.

set The unit of scoring that is next higher than a game. A set is scored when one player has won at least six games by a margin of two games.

set point The situation in which a player who is leading will win the game and with it the set by winning the next point.

sideline The line at either side of the court that marks the boundary of the playing area.

sidespin Spin imparted to the ball that causes it to rotate from one side to the other and bounce abruptly to one side when it touches the ground.

singles A form of play in which one player competes directly against another player.

slice A stroke in which sidespin is imparted to the ball.

smash A hard overhand stroke.

stop volley A swiftly hit volley that sends the ball just over the net short of the opponent's reach.

stroke The act of hitting the ball with the racket.

sudden death (See tiebreaker.)

tape The narrow band of canvas that runs along the top of the net.

tennis elbow Inflammation and swelling on the outer side of the elbow joint, usually resulting from torn muscle fibers.

30 The second point made by a player in a game.

throat The part of the racket where the head meets the handle.

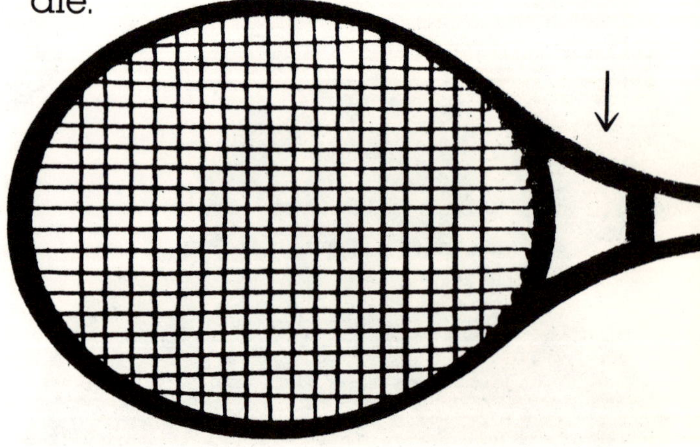

tiebreaker A period of extra play to break a tie that terminates when one player reaches a predetermined score, usually 9 or 12 points.

topspin Forward spin imparted to the ball that causes it to move downward in flight and to take a low bounce when it hits the ground.

twist The spin given a ball.

umpire The official who is positioned high above one end of the net to observe the action on both sides of the net. The umpire keeps and announces the score, indicates faults (with the assistance of the linesman) and, in general, conducts the match.

USTA Abbreviation for United States Tennis Association.

volley To return the ball before it hits the ground.

Western grip A method of gripping the racket in which the palm is more toward the bottom of the handle.

wood shot A shot in which the ball is hit accidentally with the racket frame.

96

MIXED DOUBLES

Keep the Ball in Play